HOT LICKS
FOR BLUEGRASS BANJO

HOT LICKS
FOR BLUEGRASS BANJO

by Tony Trischka

Oak Publications
New York • London • Sydney

This book is lovingly dedicated to John Trischka, Aurora Trischka, and Dede Wyland with special thanks to Jason Shulman and an appreciation to Mark-Age.

Photo Credits

page

6   Phil Straw, courtesy *Bluegrass Unlimited*
8   Courtesy Toby Stroud and *Bluegrass Unlimited*
11   Moishe Mark
86   Peter V. Kuykendall, courtesy *Bluegrass Unlimited*
120 Phil Straw, courtesy *Bluegrass Unlimited*
122 Phil Straw, courtesy *Bluegrass Unlimited*
124 David Gahr
126 Jim Erickson
128 Larry Shirley
130 David Gahr
132 Allan Finkelman
134 Eric Weber
137 Joe McHugh
140 David Gahr
141 Moishe Mark

Book design by Nina Clayton
Cover design by Tim Metevier
Edited by Peter Pickow

U.S./International Standard Book Number: 0-8256-0288-2
U.K./International Standard Book Number: 0-7119-0279-8

Distributed throughout the world by Music Sales Corporation:
799 Broadway, New York 10003
78 Newman Street, London W1P 3LA
27 Clarendon Street, Artarmon, Sydney, NSW 2064

Contents

Earl Scruggs

Preface

When I was first asked to write this book, I thought it would be a fairly straightforward task—take maybe two months tops. I'd just throw together some of my favorite licks and get on with the next project. Needless to say, it didn't turn out quite that way. Two months stretched to two years and a few of my choice licks became 650 licks of every possible description ranging from straight Scruggs to single-string bebop.

Also, the somewhat amorphous tome that I'd originally intended crystallized into a structured work, divided as follows: Scruggs, Melodic, Single-String, and an added Celebrity Section featuring the licks of such luminaries as Don Reno, J.D. Crowe, Alan Munde, and Bill Keith. Within those areas I decided that further organization was necessary. So I categorized each according to G, C, D, F, and A licks, those being the most commonly used chords in the bluegrass idiom.

In terms of goals, my plan was twofold: first, to help you build a comprehensive repertoire of licks and second, to expand your view of the banjo's capabilities. To help the flow I began each section with fairly basic licks and then moved outward from there.

My hope, then, is that you'll latch onto a number of these licks, memorize them and incorporate them into your playing. The ones that you discard as being unsuited to your musical personality may still subliminally serve you by triggering new creative thoughts. In either case—dive in, absorb, and enjoy.

Don Reno in the early fifties

Tablature

These days, a torrent of tablature is flooding the banjo market. In that out-pouring there have been a number of similar yet subtly different systems of notation. I'd like to take a moment to explain mine. We'll begin with a *measure*:

The vertical lines on either side are called *bar lines*. (Measures also appear under the *nom de plume* 'bar'.) Conveniently, each horizontal line represents a string of the banjo, the top line being the first and on down to the fifth.

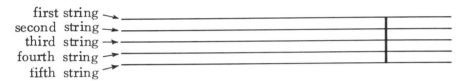

You won't be dealing with notes *per se*, but rather with numbers. This lone *3* resting comfortably on the top line

indicates that you should play the 3rd fret of the first string. A *0* on the third line

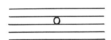

represents the open third string.

Of course, these numbers (notes) have to be organized and that brings us to the subject of *time*—$\frac{4}{4}$ time to be exact. When working out of a $\frac{4}{4}$ format you'll need four *quarter-notes* per measure ($\frac{2}{4}$ time requires two quarter-notes, $\frac{3}{8}$ time three eighth-notes, and so forth). In this tablature, quarter notes are indicated by a single line descending from the number. Here are four quarter-notes.

Although you'll be picking your fair share of quarter notes, you'll more often be dealing with *eighth notes*. Keep in mind that there are two eighth-notes to every quarter (eighth notes are played twice as fast as quarters). So if you have four quarter-notes in a measure, the equivalent would be eight eighth-notes:

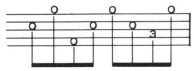

The single horizontal line connecting each group of four indicates eighth notes. A double connecting line represents *sixteenth notes* (one eighth-note = two sixteenths).

Here's a simple chart to summarize the time relationships between quarter notes, eighth notes, and sixteenths.

quarter notes

eighth notes

sixteenth notes

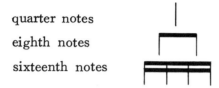

In many cases, quarter notes, eighth notes, and sixteenth notes will be combined in a single measure.

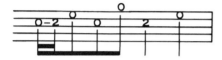

There are also certain occasions when a quarter note will be allowed to ring for twice its value. This will be indicated by a curved line connecting two quarter-notes. (Only the first should be picked.)

There's one other time element I haven't discussed yet and that's the *rest*. A rest is a period of time during which no note is being sounded. In this book I'll indicate rests by an *x* on the middle line.

This means that you should skip the time value of one eighth-note before beginning to play.

As for the right hand instructions, they're located directly under each note.
    T = thumb
    1 = index finger
    2 = middle finger
Armed with this knowledge, try

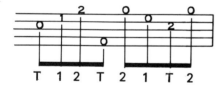

Now add these ingredients:
P = pulloff
H = hammer-on
S = slide

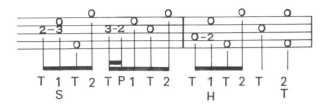

Before we begin, there's one final detail to be discussed—the *choke*. The most common choke is the 10th-fret choke (sometimes referred to as the 'diggy-diggy'). This has been immortalized by both Earl Scruggs and Ralph Stanley and will be represented by an arrow extending upward from the note.

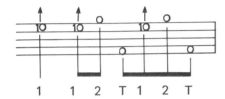

Of course other notes can also be choked as this blues passage demonstrates.

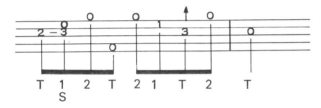

Now we begin.

Sonny Osborne

Scruggs Licks and Beyond

How Licks Work

Scruggs licks are largely based on a small number of building blocks which can be extended or combined in an almost infinite variety of ways. Here are some of those building blocks divided into slides, pulloffs, and hammer-ons. (You'll find others but these make a good foundation).

SLIDES

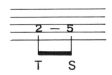 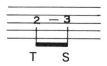 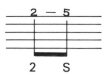

PULLOFFS

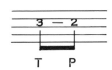 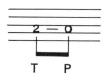 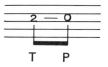

HAMMER-ONS

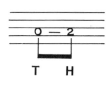 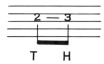 

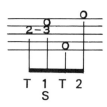

By themselves these fragments are totally one dimensional, requiring but a single motion. However, when you combine the left hand with an expanded right-hand role (roll) you can create simple Scruggs licks. Here are a few of those same building blocks integrated with rolls.

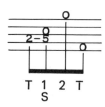 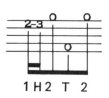

Keeping these in mind we're going to continue our progression to the larger conception—complete breaks. As I see it, licks serve two functions: to delineate a particular melody or to fill a chordal space. Let's talk first about melody. Here's "Twinkle, Twinkle Little Star" to illustrate.

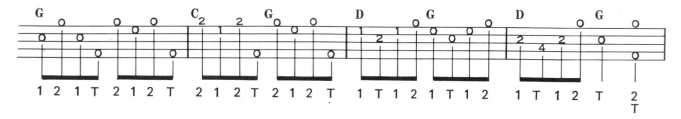

Although the melody is being embellished by characteristic bluegrass rolls, the overall sound falls just short of Scruggs style. However, if we flesh out the same tune with a few of the licks listed above the results are much more convincing.

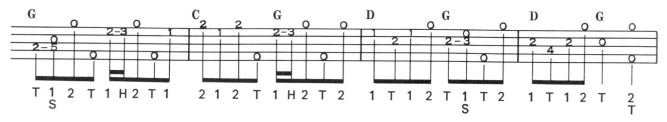

The melody is there, but now it's tucked into the slides and hammer-ons of Scruggs style rather than being baldly presented in the simple alternation of fretted and open strings. In short, the difference is in the left hand. If you'll look at the very first slide you'll see what I mean. You're playing a 2 to 5 slide on the fourth string. As it turns out, the melody note is the second of the two notes, the 5th fret of the fourth string. This is reinforced by simultaneously playing the open third string, a unison note. So you're sliding up to the melody note. Now turn back to the ten building blocks for a moment. In almost all cases the second of the two notes serves as a melody note, so you're either hammering on to it, pulling off to it, or sliding up to it. The one exception to the second-note melody rule is the 2 to 3 slide which appears in the third measure of "Twinkle, Twinkle Little Star." Although the indication is 3, I don't emphasize this note because of the discord it creates between the second and third strings. Instead I prefer to lift off my middle finger as soon as I cross the 2nd fret of the third string. This implies movement to the 4th fret (the actual melody note). The effect is enhanced by simultaneously playing the open second string, the unison of the 4th fret, third string.

We've been talking about licks as they serve the melody. Now we're going to turn to licks as they serve to fill chordal space. Perhaps "filling space" is a somewhat pejorative way of putting it, but in essence, that's what a lot of improvising is about, whether you're playing bluegrass, jazz, or an eighteenth-century baroque cadenza.

As I already mentioned, you can improvise off of the melody, and in traditional bluegrass that's a very common practice. There are times, however, when a tune won't have much of a melody (listen to "Foggy Mountain Breakdown"). On these occasions you may find yourself with a list of musical options stretching from here to Shelby, North Carolina. So how do you decide what to play? Well, the process isn't really as random as it might seem, particularly when you're dealing with Scruggs style. First of all, you should play Earl's licks as close as you can to the way he picked them back in 1956. Also, work on the spinoff licks which have evolved from his. (In other words, listen to J.D. Crowe.) Finally, make sure they fit together smoothly. No square pegs in round holes, please.

Once you get into it, you'll find that Scruggs licks in particular, and licks in general, are multipurpose modular units which can be plugged into a variety of musical situations. For instance, let's take this lick

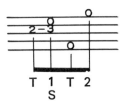

and insert it into four measures of G. That's a standard beginning form for many bluegrass instrumentals (i.e., "Foggy Mountain Breakdown," "Bluegrass Breakdown," "Lonesome Road Blues").

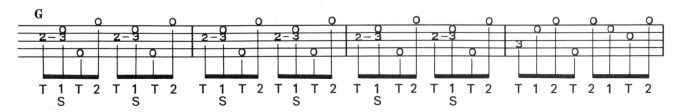

Now that gets a bit tedious after the fourth or fifth slide, so let's mix it up by introducing another time-tested Scruggs lick.

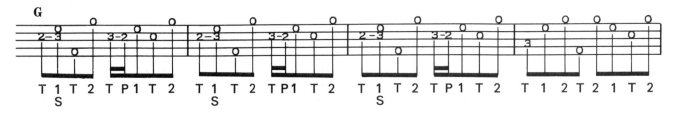

That's closer, but it still feels stiff. Add a hammer-on in the second measure.

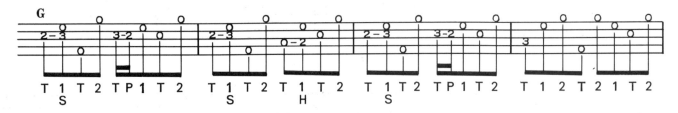

Right there you have the first four measures of "Shuckin' the Corn," and that works. Of course it's more composed than improvised, but it demonstrates lick substitution at work. We can go one step further and get an improvised feel by borrowing the signature lick to "Foggy Mountain Breakdown" and inserting it in measure two.

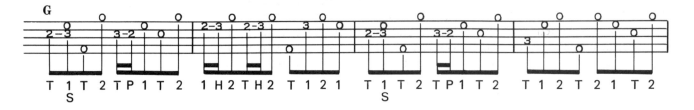

14

If we keep most of that and rework measure three, we get another improvisation.

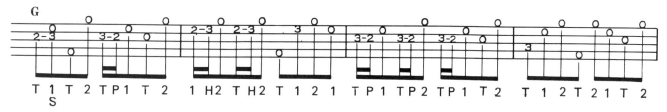

This demonstrates just a few of the infinite ways you can fill out four measures of G. And that's one of the basic challenges of Scruggs style—finding new ways to rework time-worn licks.

In many ways Scruggs style is a closed system—your raw materials (the basic building blocks) are preset—but within those limitations there's a lot of leeway. In the rest of this section we'll explore the possibilities.

Let's start with the open-G position since that's the place the majority of Scruggs licks call home. I'll be including G, C, D, and later on F and A licks, since those chords come up most often. Rather than just letting go with a geyser of licks, I'm going to organize them around the general form of "Lonesome Road Blues." In other words there will be one lead-in measure, four measures of G, two of C, two connective measures of G, two more of C, two more measures of G (linking the C and D), two measures of D, and one or two measures of tag endings in G.

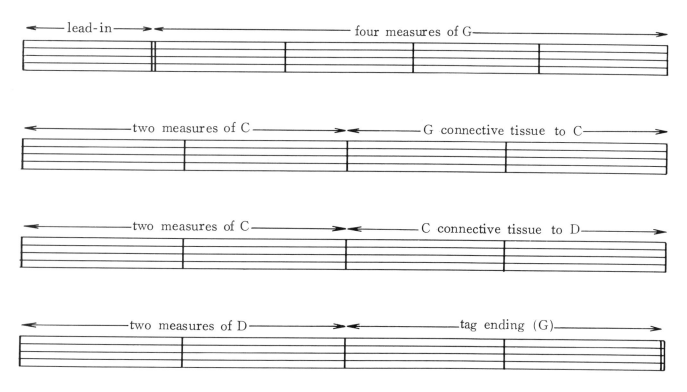

There are other basic forms, but you should have no trouble lifting licks from this one to fit the others. The thing to remember when stringing these licks together is appropriateness: The licks have to fit together seamlessly. I remember being totally in the dark the first time I heard Scruggs style. I couldn't find the logic behind those rippling sounds. It was hard to tell where one lick ended and the next one started. That won't be a problem here, because in the pages that follow it will all become very clear. To help you connect your licks I'll sometimes go two or three notes into the next measure to give you an idea of what can come next.

One more note. Bluegrass banjo playing isn't all licks. Sometimes there are measures of strict melody-oriented playing; or other, less defined chordal dog-paddling; neither of which really fits the category of licks. However, licks are at the heart of Scruggs style. So let's go back to the "Lonesome Road Blues" formula, and begin with some lead-ins.

LEAD-IN LICKS

Though some of the licks that follow are similar in nature, each has a unique shade of meaning. For instance, you have the choice of playing straightforward single-note lead-ins. (That's the way Earl likes to do it.) Or you can combine the same notes with a droning first or fifth string.

The first seventeen licks are simple and to the point. They serve as lead-ins to the first important melody note of a chosen tune. The last lick, however, stands apart. It's a micro-Scruggs composition that makes its own statement while kicking you into high gear for tunes like "Foggy Mountain Breakdown" and "Bluegrass Breakdown."

Leading into the open fourth string (D)
Suitable for "I Saw the Light":

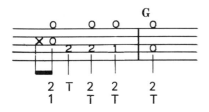 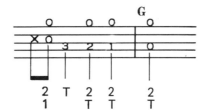

Leading into the open third string (G)
The first two work on "Salt Creek":

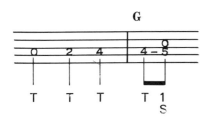 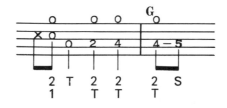

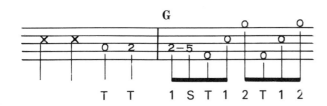

The three preceding licks have ascended to the G note. This one descends. (This can be used to start off "Whose Shoulder Will You Cry On?")

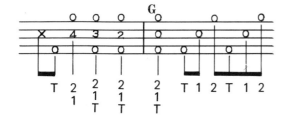

Leading into the open second string (B)
Try these on "Big Ben," "Shuckin' the Corn," and "You are My Sunshine."

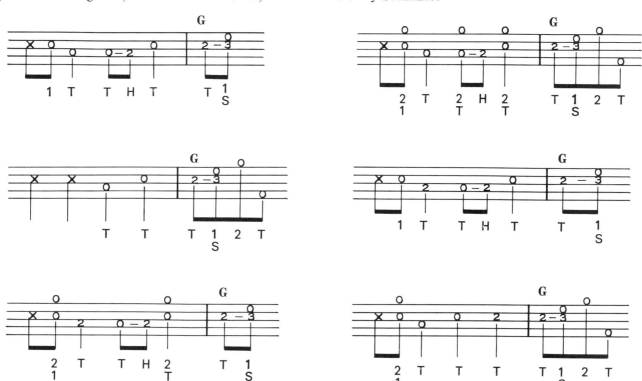

Here's a descending lick that goes well with "Down Yonder."

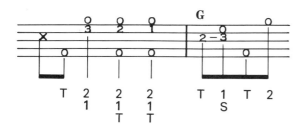

Leading into the open first string (D)

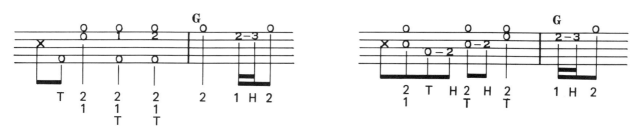

Leading into the open fifth string (G)
These work for "The Prisoners Song" and "John Henry."

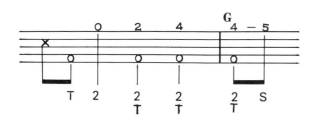 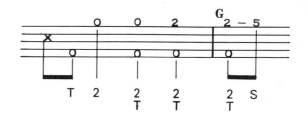

As I mentioned above, this final lead-in works for a number of hot, pulverizing banjo tunes.

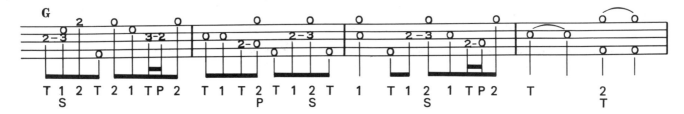

FOUR MEASURES OF G

The licks that will fill these measures have several properties. Some can be dissected into two two-measure licks or four one-measure licks, while others maintain a complete structural integrity of four measures. We'll start with the basic "Foggy Mountain Breakdown" lick (going to C at the end instead of E minor) and use that as our foundation.

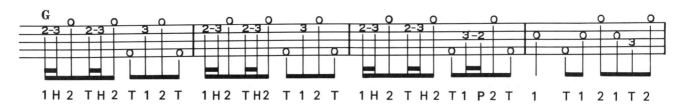

Although that's a complete thought, you could lop off the last measure and substitute one of the following in its place

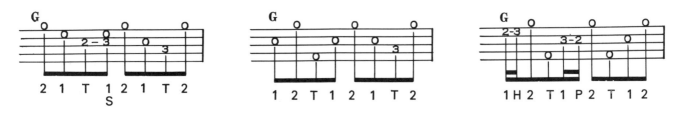

That should give you more of a feeling for the modular nature of this style.

From here we can go to four spin-off licks that begin with the "Foggy Mountain Breakdown" lick and evolve from there.

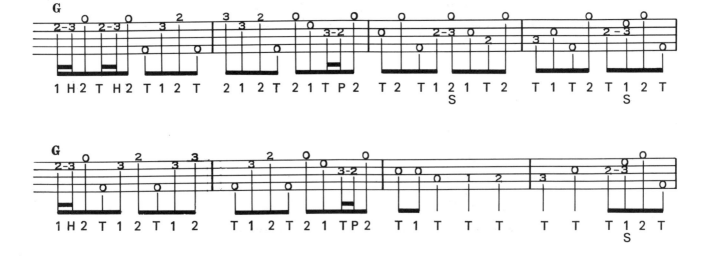

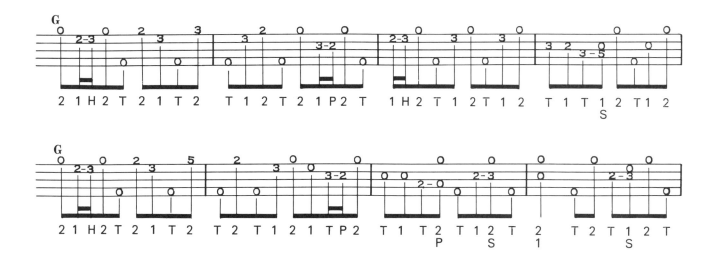

This next one is a high-neck Scruggs lick moved down twelve frets.

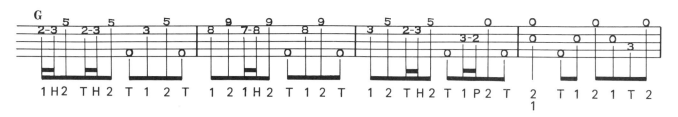

Modular mayhem:

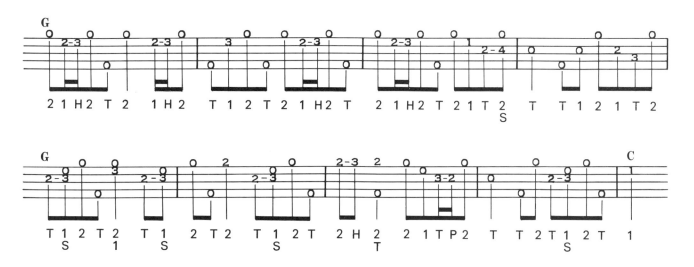

Watch the timing on the second of these next two.

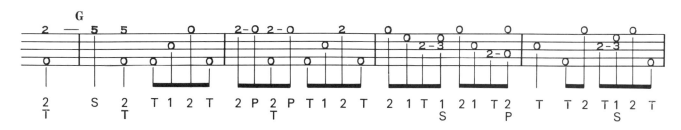

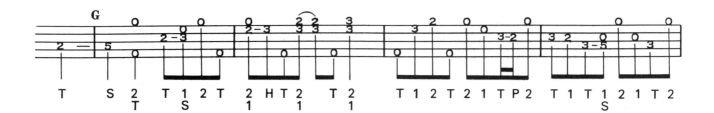

When playing the 1st fret of the second string let it ring for just a fraction of a second, then lift off. (This sharp attack is called *staccato*.)

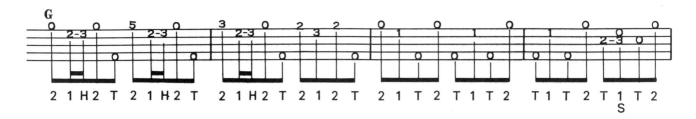

Two blues licks:

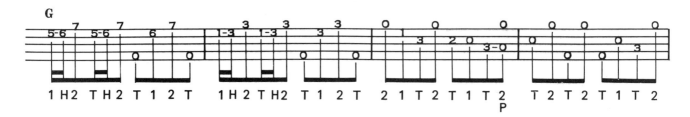

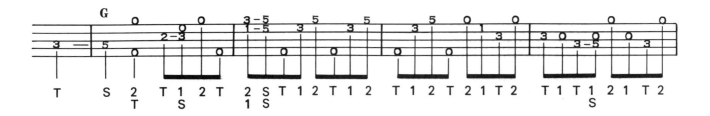

The first two measures of this next one are somewhat obscure, though not without charm. Slide first with the ring finger, using your index for the 2nd fret, first string. Then move the whole position up one fret (without lifting a finger) for the next slide. The last two measures return you to a more traditional milieu.

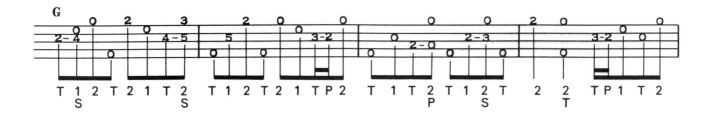

20

This is my interpretation of a lick that Ralph Stanley might, but probably never would, play. Notice the characteristic Stanleyesque index lead integrated into the forward rolls of measures three and four.

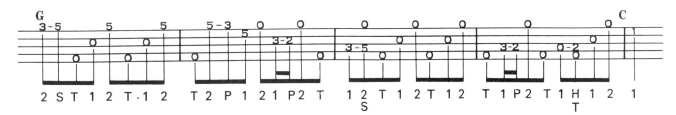

TWO MEASURES OF C

All of the preceding G licks have been leading up to this section. Sail these seven Cs for starters.

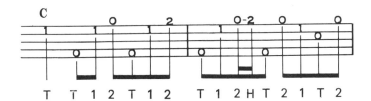

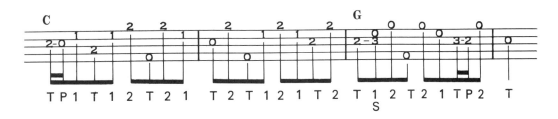

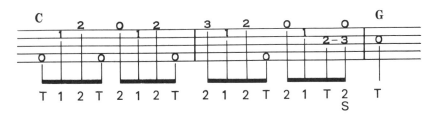

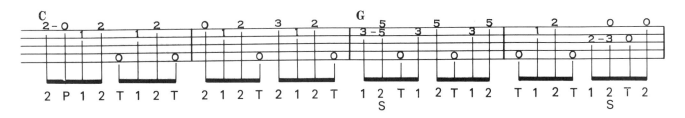

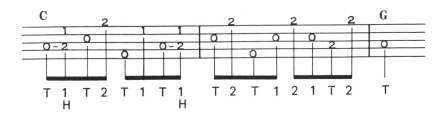

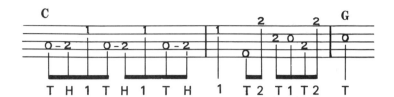

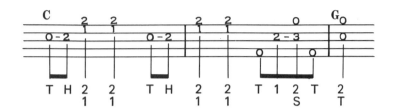

The next two are inspired by J.D. Crowe.

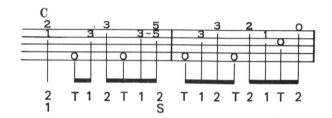

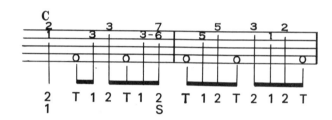

The universal "Foggy Mountain Breakdown" right-hand roll strikes again.

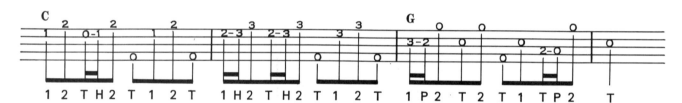

Two variations on a C7. (Use your ring finger on the 3rd fret, third string.)

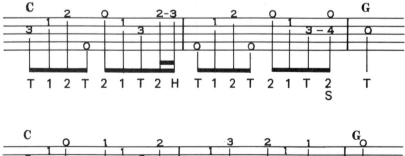

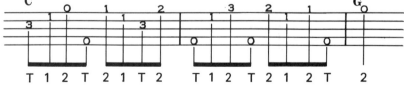

Here's a syncopated seventh. Fret the 3rd fret of the first string by barring across the first three strings.

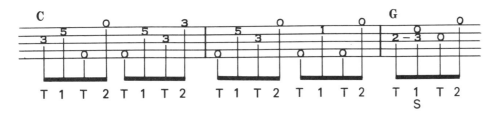

Low and inside:

The first of these two licks moves down chromatically. I threw in the second to demonstrate how the same idea could be applied elsewhere on the neck. Make up a couple of your own using the same left- and right-hand patterns.

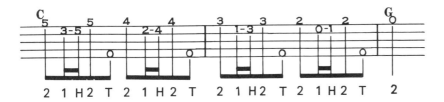

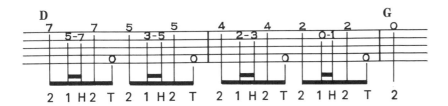

A somewhat unusual forward rolled C7 lick:

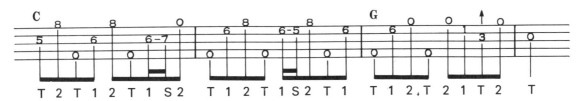

Here's a blues lick, working on the inside strings.

A syncopated C as it would lead into G and on into D:

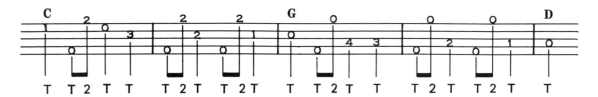

Anticipation:

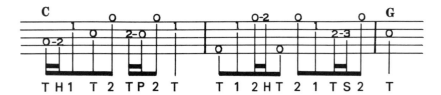

We'll finish with a few of my favorite straight-ahead Scruggs licks.

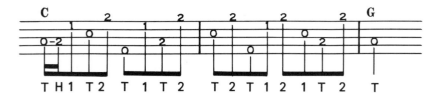

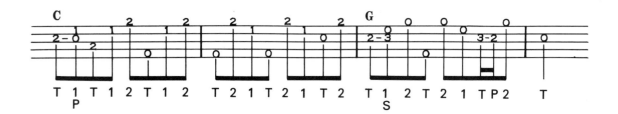

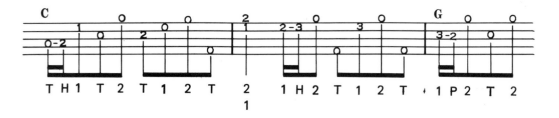

CONNECTIVE TISSUE: G to C

Continuing with the formula for "Lonesome Road Blues" we find a two-measure G gap waiting to be filled. The hot-lick potential for these bars is usually considered to be low. As its name implies, it's a somewhat gray area that falls between the two more important lick centers of C. Therefore, most of the licks here are of a more functional nature. However, as other licks will bear out, it is possible to catch the ear through here. Note: With the alteration of a few notes, many of these licks can also serve as links between C and D.

C to C

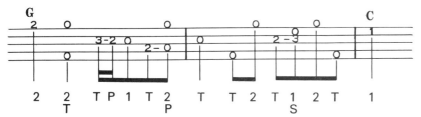

C to D

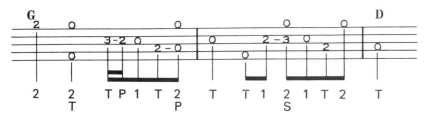

As in the above case, most of the alterations come in the second of the two measures. If you're fairly familiar with the Scruggs idiom you'll probably be able to come up with your own. If not, the G-to-D connectors will be discussed in the following section. Now try these:

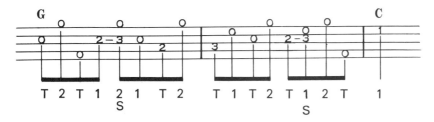

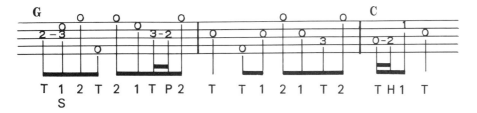

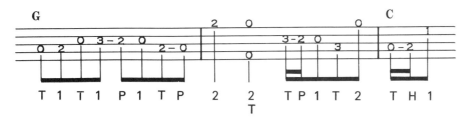

The repetition of forward rolls in the next two licks creates an even contour of line which seems to shorten the distance between the two Cs.

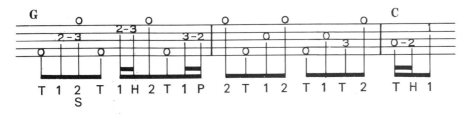

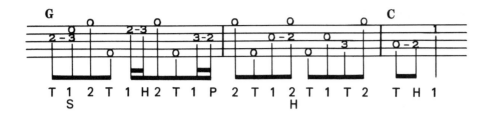

Notice the diverging lines in measure two.

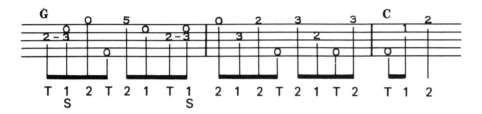

Here's a highly syncopated and convoluted lick which I carry through the C in order to create a unit of concept. This one is not easy but once you get it down it really sounds great.

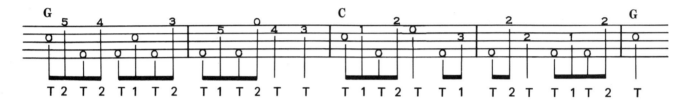

More playing to the inside:

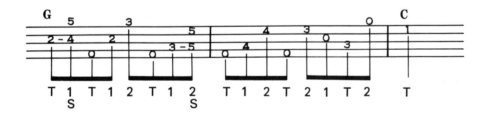

And in closing:

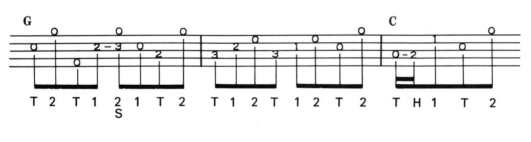

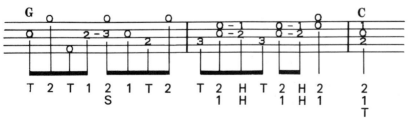

TWO MEASURES OF C

As we continue with the formula for "Lonesome Road Blues" we find two more measures of C. For these I'll refer you back to the preceding C section.

CONNECTIVE TISSUE: G to D

Here are seven licks that will connect C to D via G.

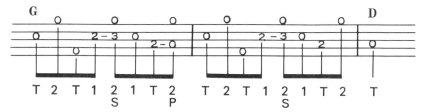

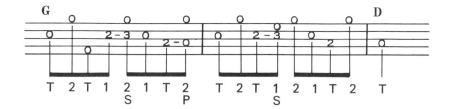

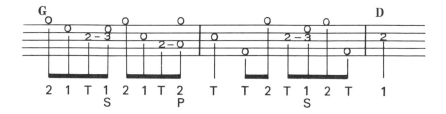

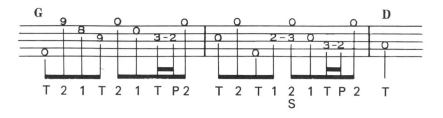

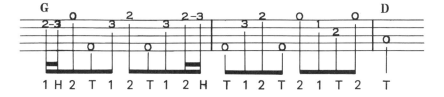

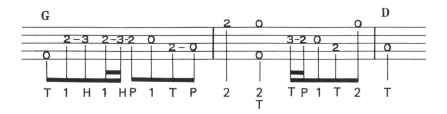

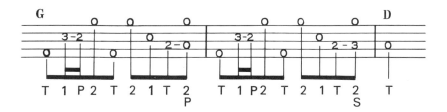

TWO MEASURES OF D

D licks, like C licks, are a ball to make up. I probably could have finished out the rest of the book with just this section. We'll start in familiar territory and then move into more uncharted realms.

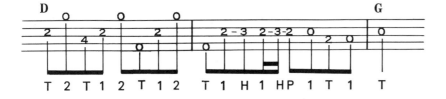

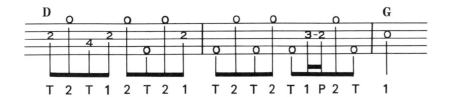

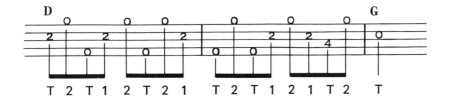

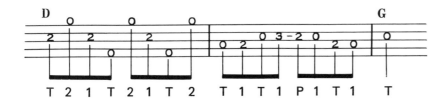

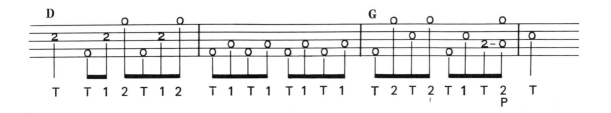

Here are two of a similar persuasion.

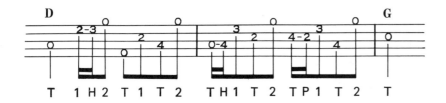

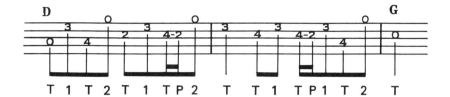

Another area of lick development derives from the basic "Foggy Mountain Breakdown" lick. Although usually associated with the key of G it also works in D because the hammer-on creates a unison D-note with the first string. This first lick is classic Scruggs.

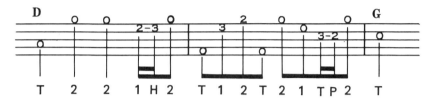

By changing the first note to an eighth note and slightly altering the rest of the first measure you get this syncopated variation.

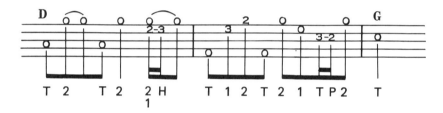

Here are some more possibilities from the same bag . . . with thanks to Bill Keith for the last lick in the series and to a displaced "Old Joe Clark" for the first.

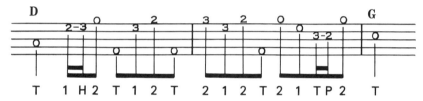

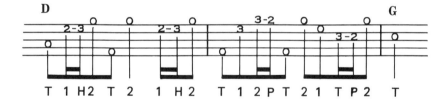

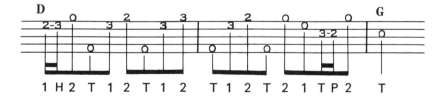

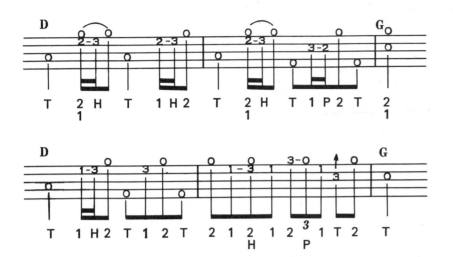

Try this punchy lick adapted from the playing of Lamar Grier. (This is a good way to anticipate the G chord.)

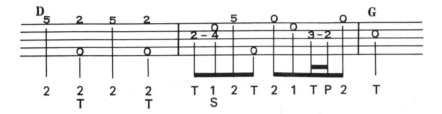

The two-note alternation in the second measure of this next lick is an effective technique for building excitement in your playing.

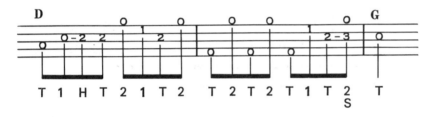

Keep the forward roll going while you hammer your way on up the neck.

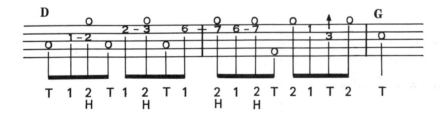

For each position in the following lick keep your ring finger moving along the first string and work from there.

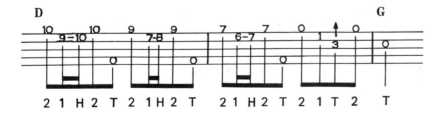

Here's a poignant one. Use your pinky to get the hammer-on and pulloff in the second measure.

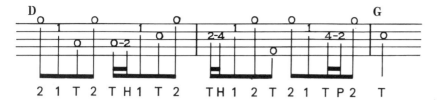

Pinky on the 4th fret, ring to middle for the pulloff:

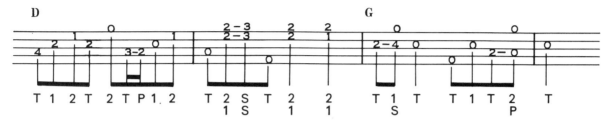

The next two have similar feels. Use the diagramed position for the first one.

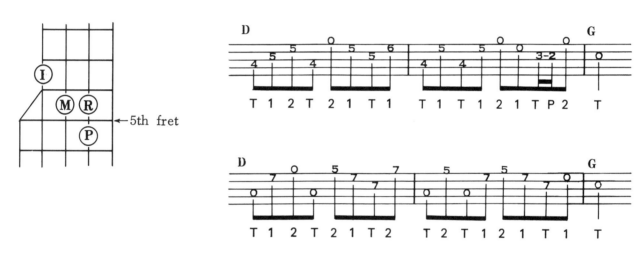

Steve Arkin once showed me a descending lick which ultimately ascended into this.

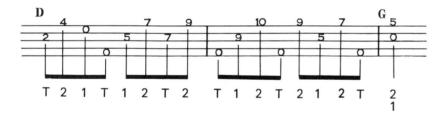

Here's one of my current favorites. It covers the fingerboard in record time.

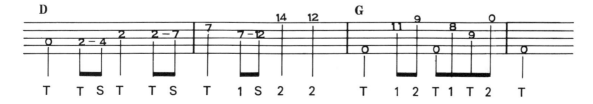

Last four then *au revoir* for D.

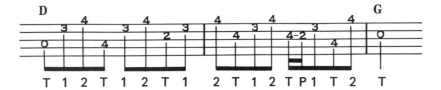

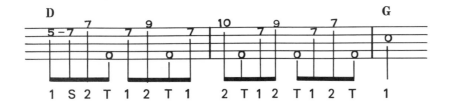

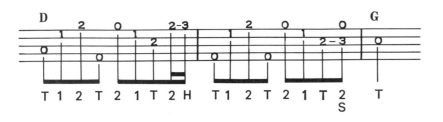

TAG ENDINGS

Tag endings serve the dual function of closing out one break and leading into another. This dead-air space usually lasts for two measures and contains no perceivable melodic content. Instead it lends itself to strict lick-oriented playing. In a moment I'll give you some examples; but first, credit goes to the boundless musical imagination of Pat Cloud for the last measure of the second to the last lick. And from our "Jumping-the-Gun Department"—the last lick features a short melodic-style passage.

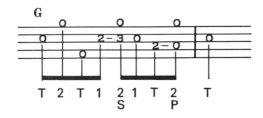

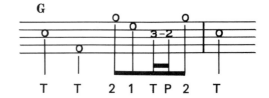

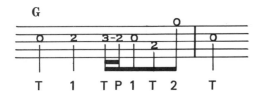

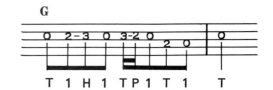

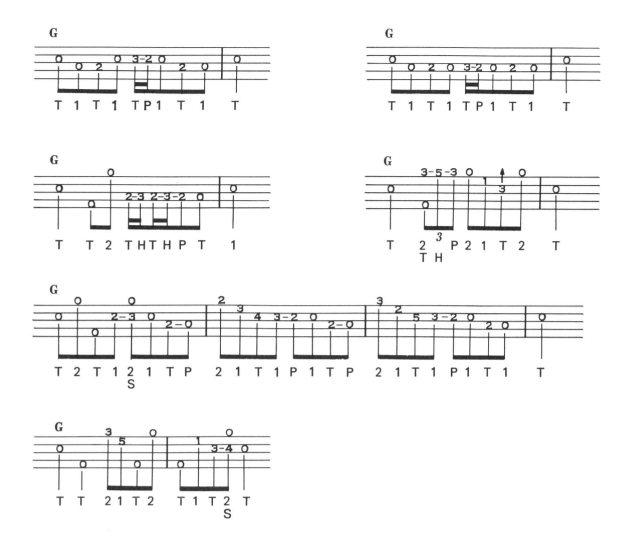

I learned the following lick from Lauck Benson, a fine picker from Albany, New York. It's his interpretation of a Ralph Stanley riff—one of those things that sounds like you've heard it 10,000 times but when you get to playing it it's brand new.

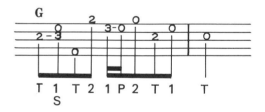

I want to close with my favorite lick. Period. This is a cosmically perfect Scruggs tag although I don't think Earl has ever played it. Thanks to Bela Fleck for transmission.

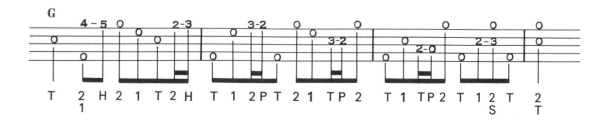

F Licks

Now that you've gone through a number of G, C, and D licks, here are some licks in F. These will come in handy for "Little Maggie," "Bluegrass Breakdown," "Theme Time," and quite a few others.

We'll start with five single-measure licks. Generally, if you're going from an F to a D chord, the first note of the next measure should be the open fourth-string. If you're heading towards, G, shoot for the open third.

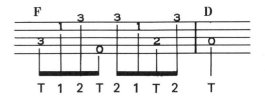

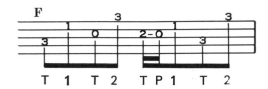

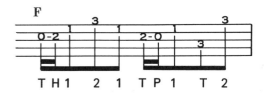

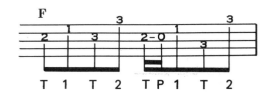

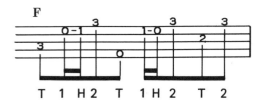

More often, you'll probably have to figure out ways to fill up two measures of F. So here are twenty suggestions ranging from fairly simple to downright difficult (but don't let that throw you).

These first two are variations on the "Foggy Mountain Breakdown" riff.

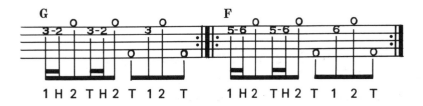

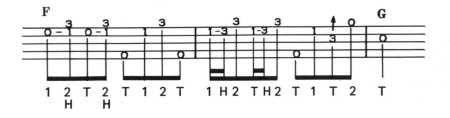

Here's another variation using pulloffs instead of hammer-ons.

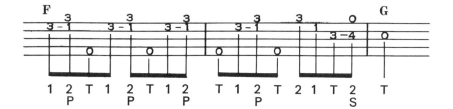

Here are two more in a somewhat Scruggsy vein.

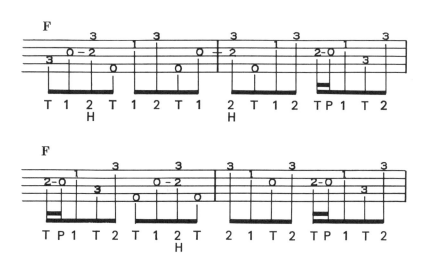

These next three licks are very simple in terms of the left hand so look to the right hand for some nice syncopation.

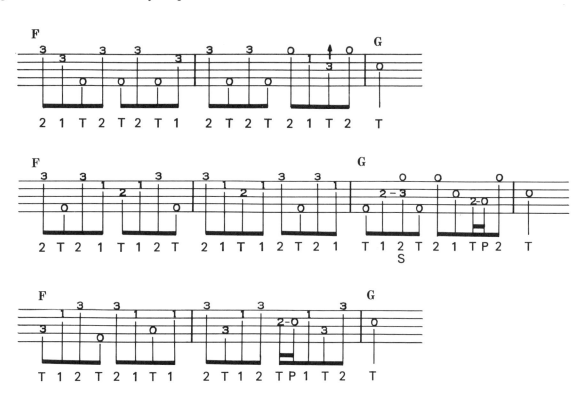

This lick combines a slightly unusual left-hand position with some forward rolling syncopation.

Here's one I use for "Bluegrass Breakdown." It's a borderline melodic lick jumping from the first to the second inversion of F. Slide with the index finger of the left hand.

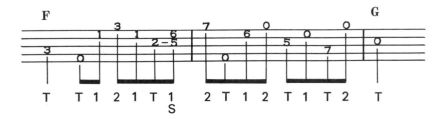

If Aaron Copland were to pick up a banjo he might come up with something like this; based on the first three inversions of F.

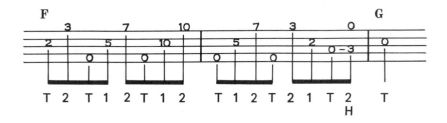

Macho style:

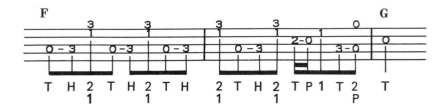

Based on a lick of Lamar Grier's:

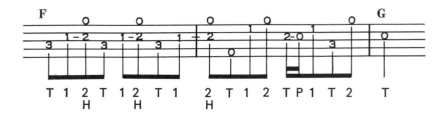

36

Descending inversions:

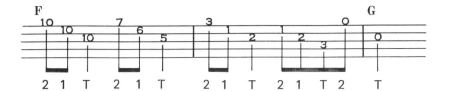

Jagged:

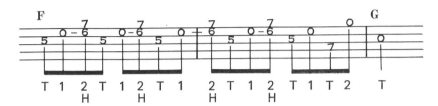

Ear stretching time: The next two licks will show you how not strictly F positions will work against an F chord. (For the first one, barre with your index finger.)

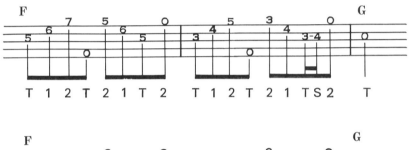

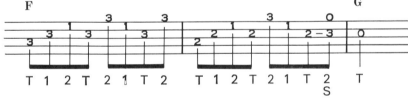

This last lick has a gently loping nature, making the most of a simple 7th-fret F position.

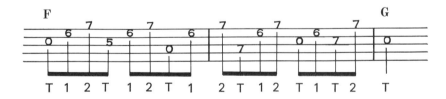

A Licks

Although A licks are somewhat less prevalent than those in F, they're still important in many bluegrass tunes. "Salty Dog" has two measures of A to fill, and Jimmy Martin's "Hit Parade of Love" has three, to name just a couple. In the following licks I'll be working out of the two-measure idiom since that seems to be the most useful format to deal with. If necessary you can whittle these licks down or expand on them, depending on your needs.

For the first lick you should use the pinky, ring, and middle fingers on the first, second, and third strings respectively. Move the middle finger to the fourth string after the pulloff.

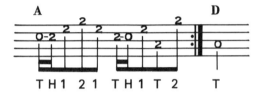

In this next lick you should barre your index finger across the first three strings at the 2nd fret, using your pinky to explore the upper frets on the first string.

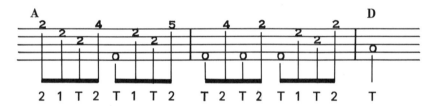

Slide up to the 7th-fret A position.

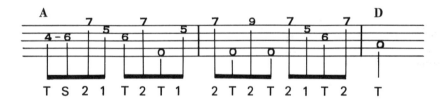

Here's another evolution of the "Foggy Mountain Breakdown" lick.

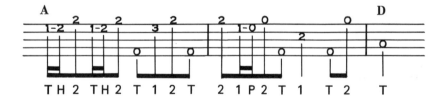

This next lick starts with an A7 position and chromaticizes towards the end.

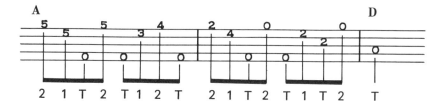

Try this slightly bluesed-out, forward rolling syncopator.

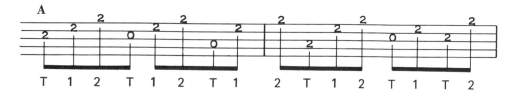

Here's a similar idea, this time utilizing backward rolls instead of forward rolls. Start with the same left-hand position you used for the first lick in this section, then barre your index finger across the first two strings at the 1st fret.

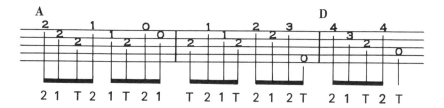

Thanks to Buck Owens for this one

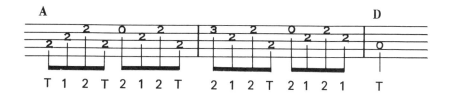

Here's a variation on "Ground Speed."

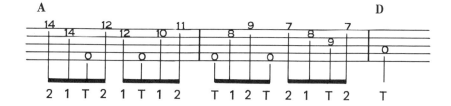

Watch the slides.

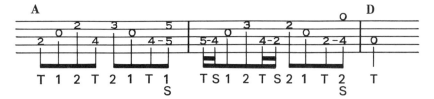

I think this is a really pretty position to work from. You can apply it to any other chord as well.

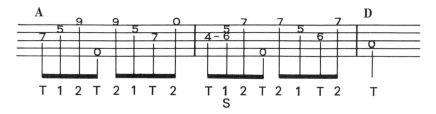

This cascade of pulloffs demonstrates how you can use open strings to good advantage while working off an A chord. The technique is reminiscent of the clawhammer style.

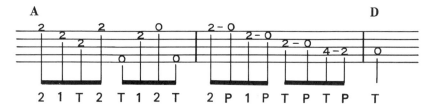

Backup

For many of you this should be the most important section in the book. You won't find a lot of "hot licks" per se. You will, however, come in contact with the basic tools to make you a stronger backup musician. Remember, if you're playing in a band a good part of your time will be spent out of the limelight, complementing the singer or the other instrumentalist(s) with whom you're alternating breaks. Part of the time you can be effective by simply playing driving, unobtrusive down-the-neck Scruggs style. (Listen to Scruggs or J.D. Crowe to get the idea.) On other occasions you'll want to move up the neck, and for that there are certain prescribed licks (and their variants) which come in handy.

Most of the licks that follow use Scruggs as a role model. And for good reason. His original backup licks, created single-handedly in the late forties and fifties, define the idiom. In almost every case they're expressions of incredible subtlety and appropriateness.

To start, we'll be working out of the 5th-fret G position. The parentheses indicate that you should damp the three notes by letting the pressure of the strings lift your fingers off the fretboard. Never let your fingers leave the strings.

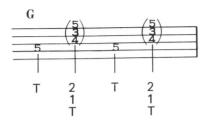

Now that you've tried it, you can hear that this is a somewhat percussive lick. As such it can fill the obsessive offbeat chunk void which is created when the mandolin takes a break. It's also a good way to keep out of a guitar player's hair if he or she is taking a break.

Here's a more swinging variation.

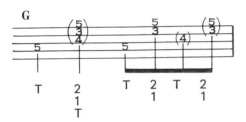

Again, the same idea, this time moving back and forth between the 5th- and 9th-fret G positions.

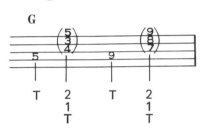

Here it is with the rhythmic variant.

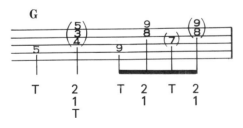

By the way, if you get into a jam (session) and don't know the chords to a tune, you can still use the above licks by simply damping all the notes.

Scruggs borrowed a lot from the swing era and this next lick comes straight from the sax section of the Glenn Miller Band.

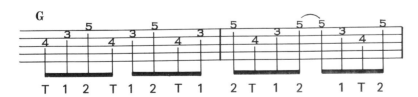

Incidentally, that lick can be moved up the neck for C, D, A, etc., and is one of the most common backup licks in all of bluegrass. Here it is an octave higher.

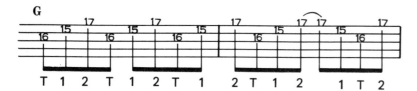

You can vary this by wrapping your thumb around the fifth string to create a G6.

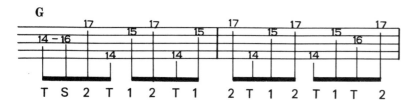

Here are two more variations in C.

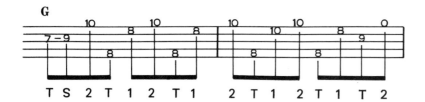

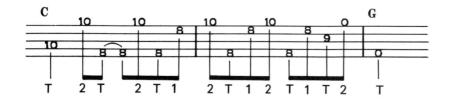

This is the same idea, but working out of a different inversion.

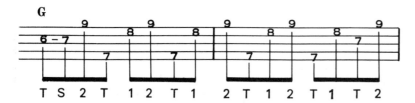

Now change it to a 7th chord to lead to C.

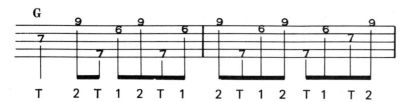

Here's another G7 position.

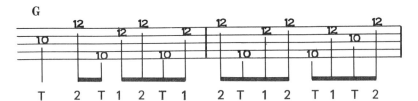

The 9th chord is a very handy, though underused, position in bluegrass. Try this.

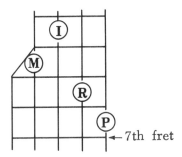

Here it is rolled. (You can move this around the neck too).

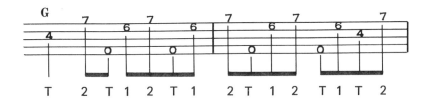

The following is an exercise to get you from G to C. It utilizes some of the positions you've just learned.

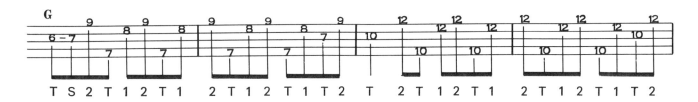

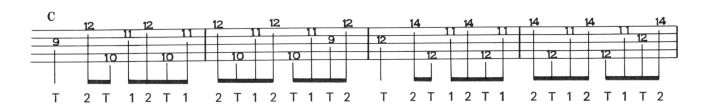

This next position is extremely important for playing lead and backup up the neck.

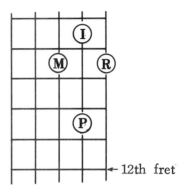

← 12th fret

Try these three manifestations.

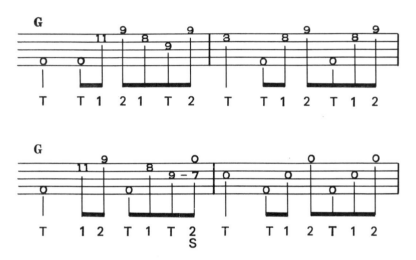

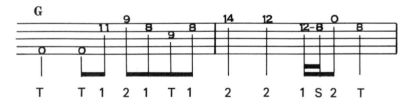

These are representative of another milieu that Scruggs varies to the hilt. The second lick represents Rudy Lyle in Manchuria.

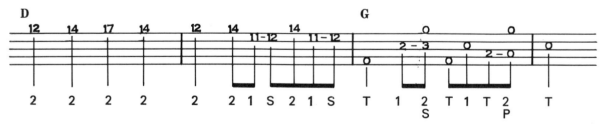

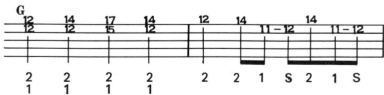

44

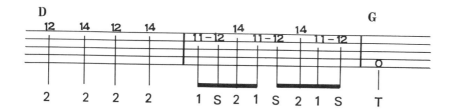

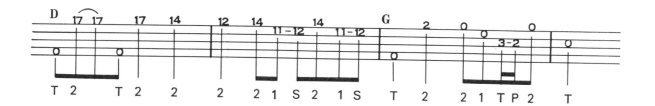

For the next three licks, (as with many of the others in this section), you should move your right hand fairly close to the point where the neck meets the pot. By doing this you'll be able to get more flow from your slides. These are all based out of the 9th-fret G position. The middle lick is taken note-for-note from a 1952 Flatt and Scruggs recording.

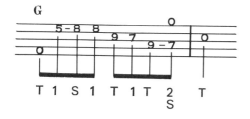

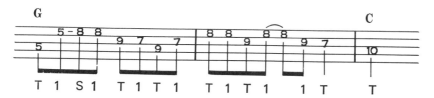

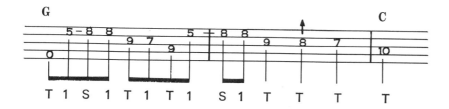

Now that you have a repertoire of licks to work with, let's put them to use. Here's how they look in the context of a standard bluegrass progression.

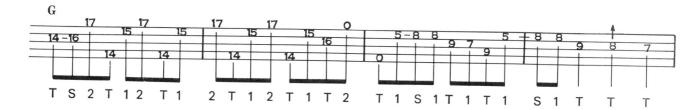

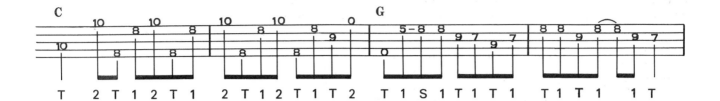

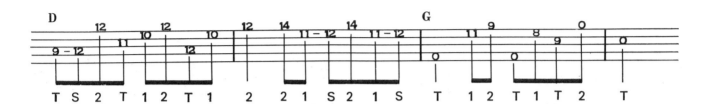

Let's go for a few more. This is a very common Scruggs lick, with minor structural considerations courtesy of Peter Schwimmer.

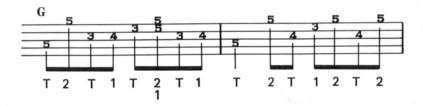

Here's an odd, but extremely effective Scruggs lick which juxtaposes a G tonality against D.

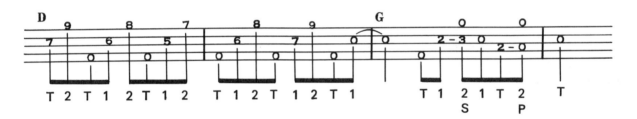

And a slightly obtuse variation, based on the playing of Lamar Grier.

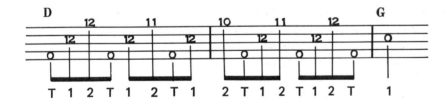

This is a syncopated, Scruggsily chromatic D lick.

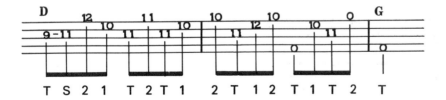

Two more wonderful swing licks taken note-for-note from early fifties Scruggs. In both cases slide up to the 9th-fret G inversion after the first note.

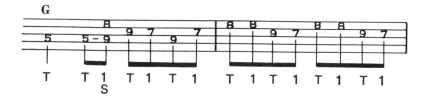

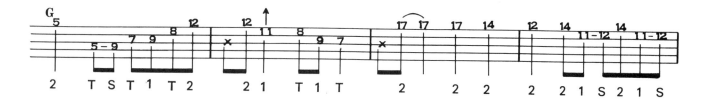

These last two licks have a strong right-hand orientation. The first comes from Allen Shelton. The second is one that I always associate with Dr. Banjo himself, Peter Wernick.

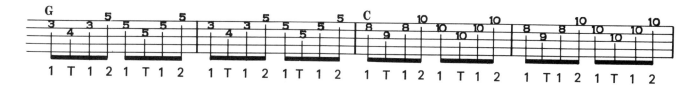

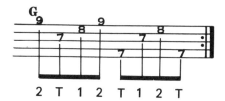

BLUES BACKUP

The blues has always played an important part in bluegrass, so it's natural that it would find its way into backup playing. The young J.D Crowe, during his stint with Jimmy Martin, developed a good number of bluesy licks, relying heavily on chokes to get his sound. The licks that follow are not necessarily note-for-note the way J.D. would play them, but they have that flavor. To get the proper feeling, put a lot of bounce in your right hand. (Technical note: an ascending arrow in the tablature indicates a choke, the dotted line indicates that you should hold the choke and the descending arrow indicates that you should release the choke.)

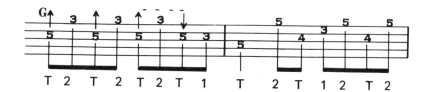

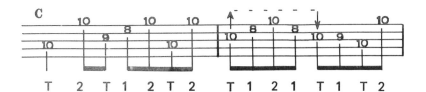

SLOW BACKUP

A slow tune is not traditionally the most advantageous setting for a banjo player. Removed from his or her natural environment of fast and medium tempo songs he or she often becomes disoriented or bored, and a state of ennui soon sets in. In hope of combating this syndrome, I'm including a short section on slow backup.

On the face of it, this first lick is dreadfully boring. But if you can adopt a certain Zen attitude towards it, you can peacefully negotiate a three minute song at a metronome reading of seventy-two. Some of Bill Monroe's banjo players have favored this lick. All power to the forward roll and the attendant mystical properties of the number three.

This next example is actually a series of licks hung on the framework of a simple three-chord bluegrass progression. It employs one of Scruggs's favorite techniques, that of alternating the index and middle fingers on the first two strings. As it turns out, this right-hand pattern is a weak point for many pickers, at least at faster tempos. If this is true for you, you might also want to look at this as an exercise, starting off slowly and then building up speed.

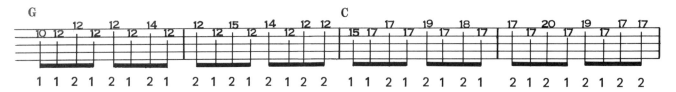

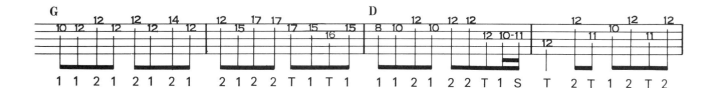

Here's a backup technique used by such pickers as Sonny Osborne and Allen Shelton. It's a chord derived style and as you can see in the following examples, it involves alternating the thumb with the index and middle fingers in a triplet rhythm. Here are three right-hand variations you'll come across.

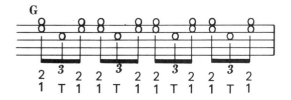

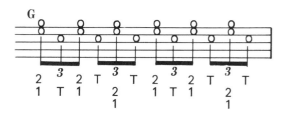

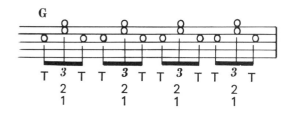

I'm not going to go into detail about the chord forms you'll be working with in this next example but see if you can apply what you find here to other chords. The D-lick at the end is one of Sonny Osborne's strokes of genius. (The first measure is shorter than the rest because it serves as a lead-in.)

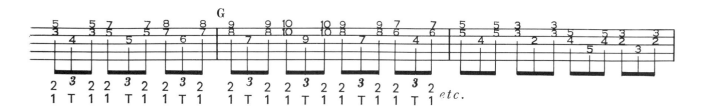

This final technique takes the previous one into another dimension. Instead of dealing with just one common inversion at a time, you'll be transinverting. That is to say you might take the bass note of one inversion and combine it with two notes of the next higher inversion. Here are some examples.

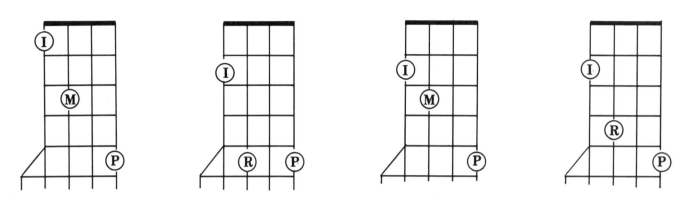

When you start putting some of these forms together the results can often be quite beautiful. In fact, the voicings are often like those of the steel guitar, a truly supernal instrument. We also have Sonny Osborne to thank for this style. To avoid confusion you should be aware that the first measure serves as a lead-in.

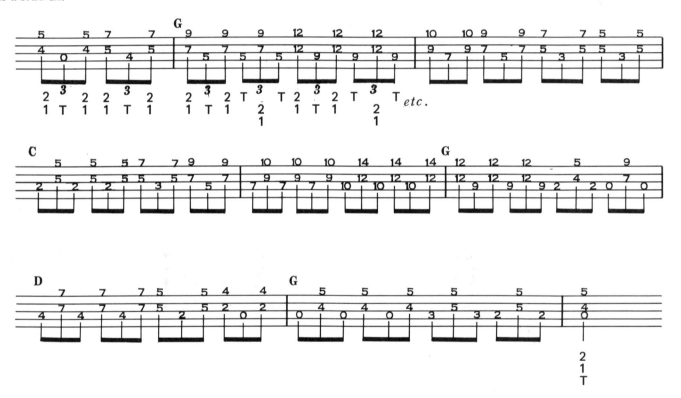

Single-String Style

Although the melodic style has opened up many possibilities for creative banjo playing and has its own set of advantages, the single-string approach is, in many ways, more versatile, particularly in terms of moveable positions and plain common sense. It's true that the single-string style is not as fluid as the melodic (due to the fact that you're often picking the same string two or three times in a row). But you will be getting more attack and drive out of your licks. Also, if you know a lick in one closed position (that is, using no open strings), you can then move it just about anywhere on the neck. There's also a logic to single-string playing that's often missing in the melodic approach. For instance, it's hard to improvise freely when you have to jump to a lower-pitched string to get a higher note.

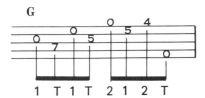

The single-string approach, on the other hand, is totally linear. If you want a higher note, you go to a higher fret on either the same or a higher-pitched string. Guitarists have been doing this for years and yet most banjo players have barely touched on the possibilities of the style.

Don Reno is almost singlehandedly responsible for introducing this approach to the bluegrass world, and until recently his repertoire of licks has stood as the primary source of single-string data. But . . . there's still much, much more that can be done. So I hope the licks that follow will steer you on an ever-expanding course of musical exploration.

G Licks in Open Position

Whereas Earl Scruggs created a world of arpeggiated chords and slow-moving melodies, the single-string style is reliant on scales and accelerated melodic lines. In fact every note can be considered a part of the melody.

To construct these melodies we must begin with scales. Let's start with G.

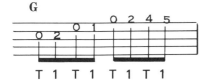

As in the above case, every single lick in this chapter should begin with the thumb of the right hand. This means the thumb will be hitting the first and fifth eighth-notes in each measure. Since these are the downbeats, or prominent beats, they benefit from the power of the downward moving thumb.

Here again is a G scale, this time with the addition of three extra scale-notes on the bottom. (Notes in parentheses indicate alternate fingerings.)

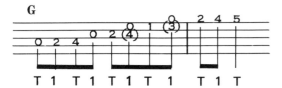

From these notes we can begin to construct licks. This first one is fairly straightforward.

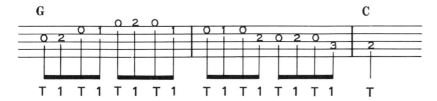

The only problem you may run into here is the crossing of the index over the thumb to get to the lower strings (beginning with the eighth note of the first measure). This is common practice in the single-string style so please be patient while your fingers adjust. Here are a few more along the same lines.

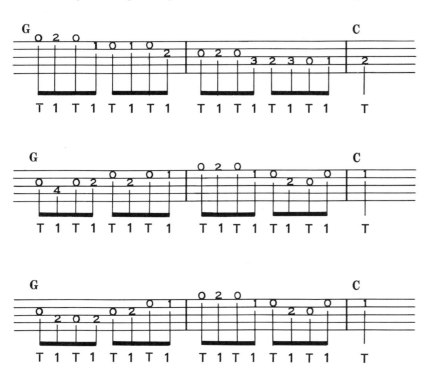

Now you may be thinking, "Why don't you just play that last lick in the melodic style? The notes fit perfectly." Well that's true. But there's a certain power and bounce that comes from the single-string style that's hard to get melodically. I think this is due, in large part, to the fact that the same notes you play melodically are often played on higher strings (those under greater pressure) in the single-string style. This has to give you more bite. Check these two examples for comparison.

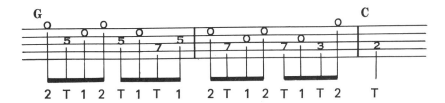

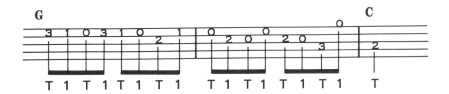

Here are two related licks that bubble their way on into C.

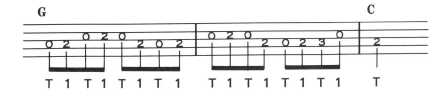

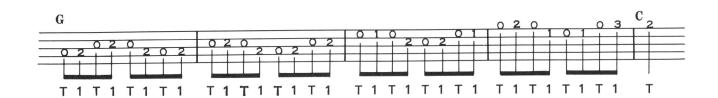

This version of "Sally Goodin" will give you a more expanded perspective on open-position single-string playing.

Sally Goodin

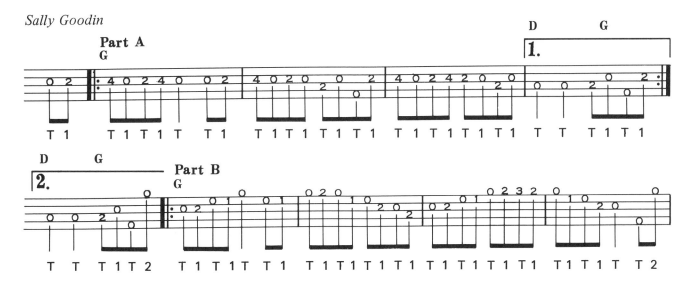

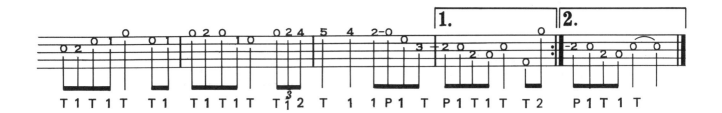

By the way, there are a number of other fiddle tunes, such as "Soldier's Joy" and "Fisher's Hornpipe" (in D) which work well in the single-string style. So you may want to investigate some of those possibilities.

To continue, here's a chromatic lick moving from G to C.

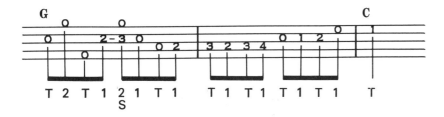

Indeed, chromatics are plentiful in the single-string approach. Check the chromatic passages in the following licks and find the hidden Flatt run.

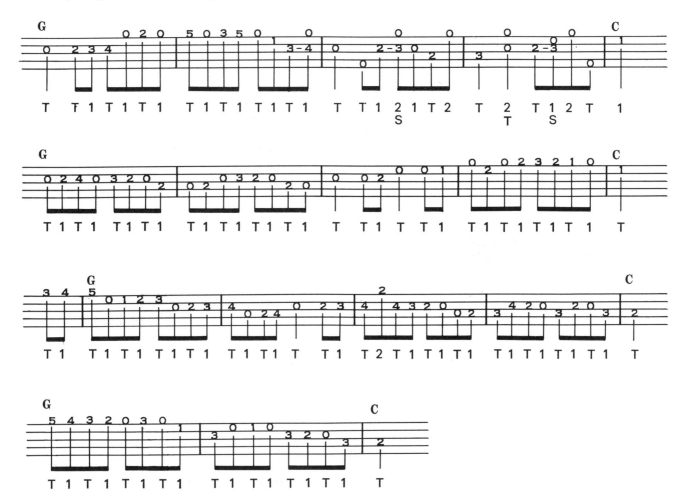

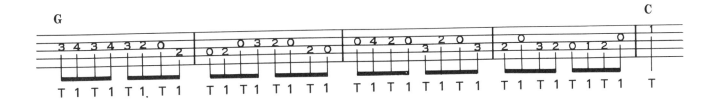

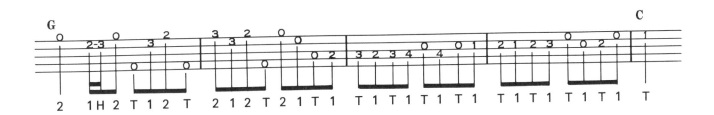

This next lick is actually two. You'll find that you'll be able to use exactly the same left-hand position for the C lick as you do for the G.

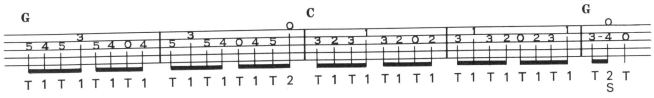

Try these two tag endings.

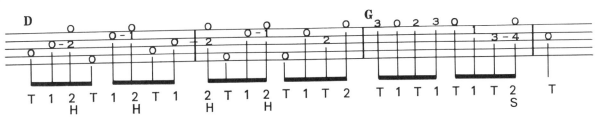

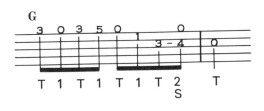

Finally, here's a slightly less than hip, albeit fun, version of "Nine-Pound Hammer." Notice the repetitive motif throughout.

Nine-Pound Hammer

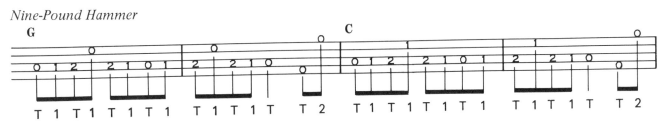

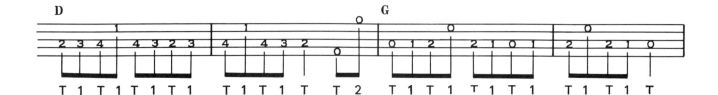

One more word: To avoid some of the choppiness inherent in the single-string style, linger on the fretted notes as long as you can before lifting your fingers to the next fret. You'll have the time to move, plus you'll have an extra margin of sustain to smooth out your solos. There are, of course, occasions when you'll want a clipped sound, but for the most part let things ring.

Closed-Position Licks

As I mentioned at the beginning of this chapter, closed positions are simply those positions which don't use open strings. As satisfying as open-string playing can be, there are strong advantages to the closed-position approach. For instance, if you can play a closed G-lick at the 5th fret, you can easily move the entire position up five half-steps to the 10th fret and use it as a C lick. By doing this, you not only compound your repertoire of licks, but you also expand your knowledge of the neck.

In the sections that follow I've organized the fingerboard according to seven distinct positions. Each one begins with a consecutive note of the G scale (i.e. the first position begins with G, the second with A, and so forth). In terms of the left hand, start every position with the index finger and then move through all of the available notes of the scale found in that position. Once you get all of this down, try the same thing starting with your middle, ring, and pinky.

FIRST POSITION
The first position is so called because it begins with the first note of the G scale, G.

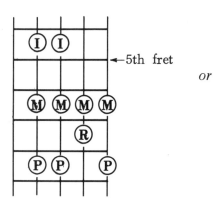
or
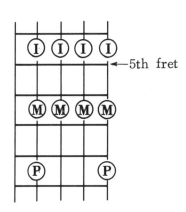

And in tablature:

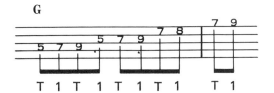 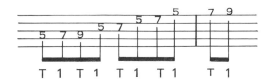

For these fingerings you'll find it best to plant your thumb directly behind the neck so that your fingers arch out over the fingerboard. This will give you a strong pivot-point from which to work. Also, notice that certain fingers are being assigned to particular frets to create optimal economy of movement . In most cases you'll use one finger per fret. In this position, since you're fanned out over five frets and have only four available fingers on the left hand, the middle finger will double on the 6th and 7th frets.

If you're like most of us, your pinky probably feels somewhat akin to a vestigial organ. But continued practice with these scales and licks will bring it around.

At first these licks may seem difficult, but give yourself a chance. If you keep with it you'll begin to move out of some of your old habitual playing and into some exciting new territory. Even if you don't memorize the licks themselves, they'll serve as exercises to free up your left hand.

Lick number one in this series moves from G to F with a nice syncopation. Notice the subtle difference in timing found within each chord.

Here's another G-to-F series suitable for "Little Maggie." The F is a carbon copy of the G lick moved down two frets.

Three blues licks:

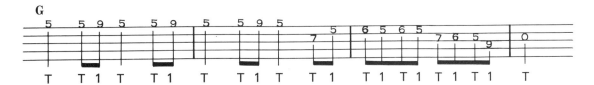

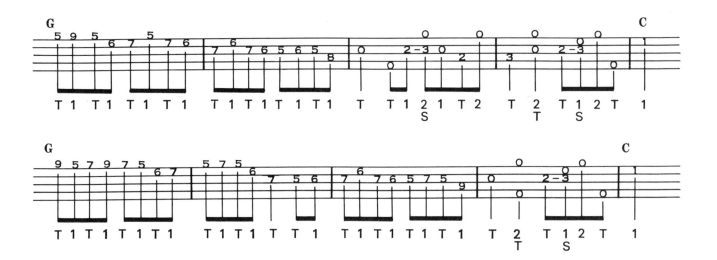

This next one is primarily ascending *à la* the melodic style, the difference being, of course, the fact that you can move it up a fret to get a G♯, or to A or B etc., etc. It will help to barre the 5th fret with your index finger.

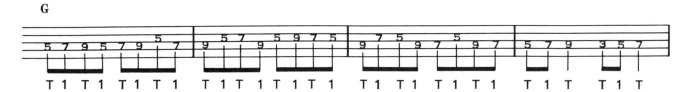

Here's an interesting tonality to play against G, then F. Again, barre with the index.

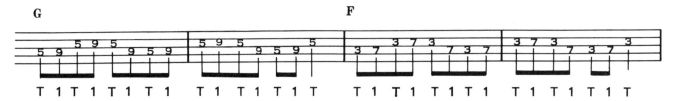

Here's a descending pattern very familiar to melodic players. Barre across the first two strings with the middle finger to get the last two notes of the first and second measure.

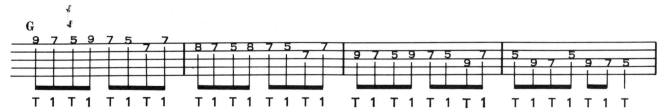

Each of the chords in the next passage features a repeating six-note pattern. At first the resulting syncopation may confuse you, but once you put some speed on it it will smooth out nicely. Work out of our first position for the G, then make minor left-hand modifications for the C and D. Be sure to keep the middle finger planted on the third string, 7th fret for the G and C, then on the third string, 5th fret for the D.

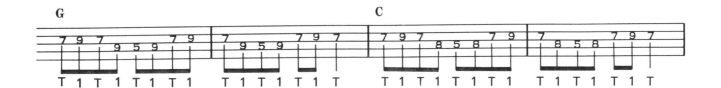

SECOND POSITION

As it's name implies, the second position starts with the second note of the G scale, A. Whereas position one spans five frets, this covers four frets. That computes to one finger per fret.

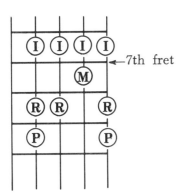 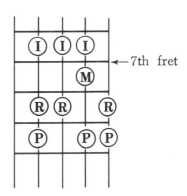

In tablature:

 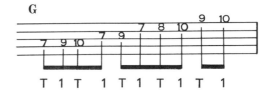

Here's Reno's building block for "Follow the Leader."

We can expand to this.

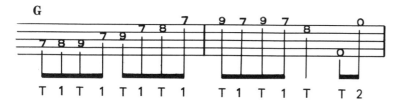

And this:

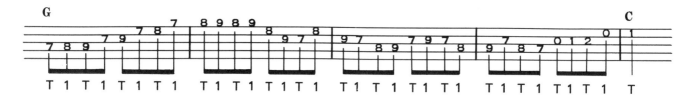

Here's another lick you can use for "Follow the Leader," I picked this up from Mike Marshall, a fine mandolin player who performs with David Grisman.

The next two licks have a similar feel in terms of syncopation. Notice the chromaticism in the second.

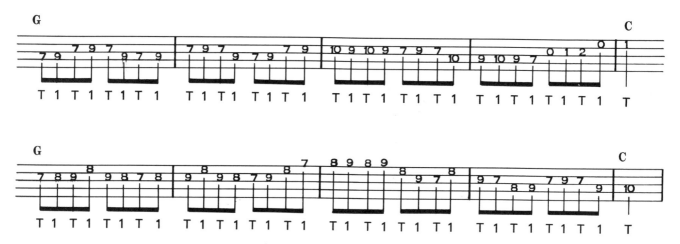

Try these pattern licks. The second one can best be executed by barring across the first two strings with your index finger.

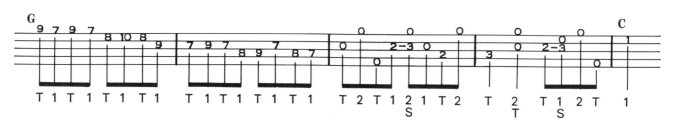

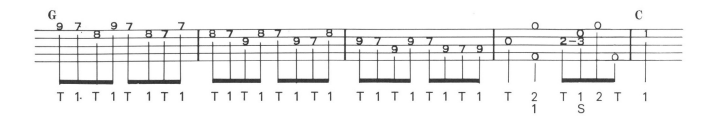

Two blues licks now. The first comes in two parts. Measures one and two are based on the position we're dealing with. The last two measures complete the thought down the neck. Play the first note with your pinky.

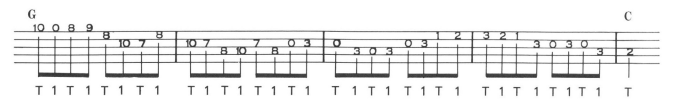

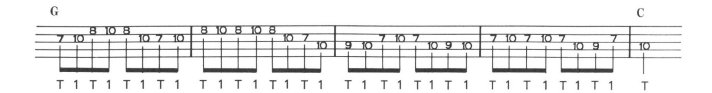

THIRD POSITION

This position begins with the third note of the G scale, B.

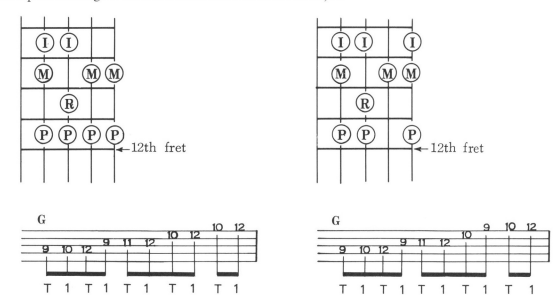

Descend to C and start with your pinky.

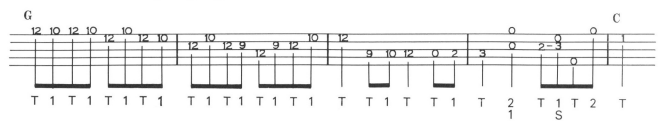

For this next one, place your pinky on the 12th fret of the first string, then jump it to the 12th fret of the third string. (You can use your ring finger on the third string if you find it easier.) Be sure to pivot off the index at the 9th fret, first string. From there you can stretch just a bit to get the C position (measures three and four).

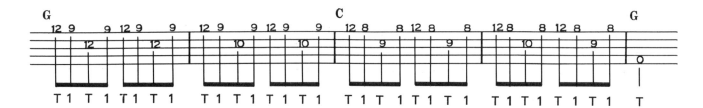

The following lick utilizes a technique which is commonly applied in jazz guitar styles. To expedite movement between two notes which are at the same fret but on different strings you can barre with the initial left-hand finger being used. For instance, in this case you should barre with the pinky to fret the third and fourth notes of measures two and three.

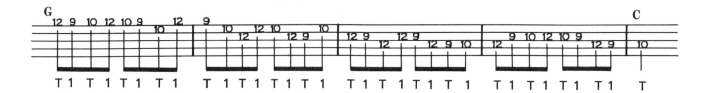

By now I think you're armed with enough knowledge to work through the rest of the licks in this section without further explanation. Remember, once you can play these out of the closed-G position you'll be able to move them around anywhere on the neck. Also, be aware that fragments of these licks can sometimes be lifted for insertion elsewhere. Use your imagination.

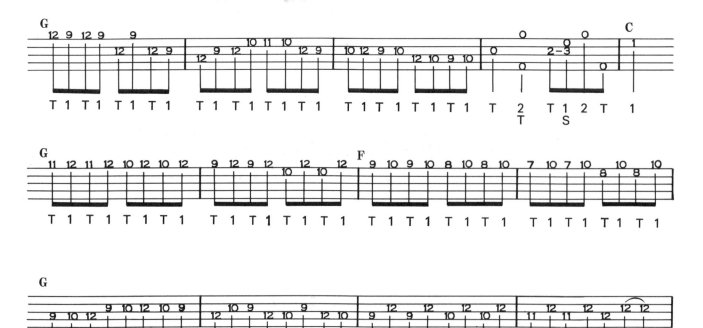

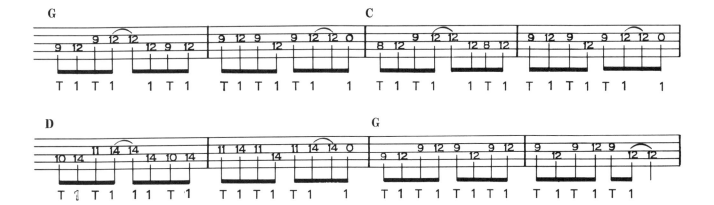

FOURTH POSITION

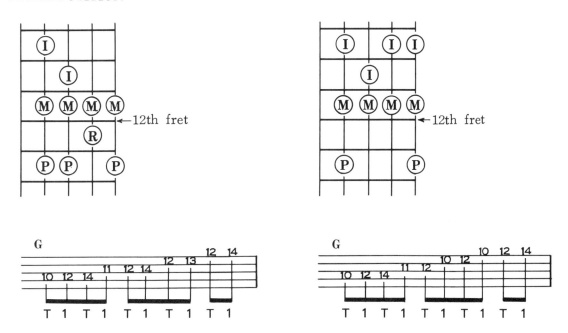

This G-to-C segment will demonstrate again the way in which you can play against two or more chords without shifting your left hand position.

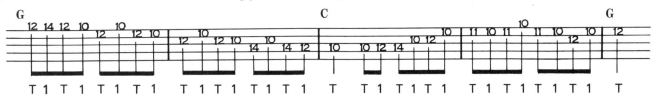

And try this slick bebop lick transferrable to D and C.

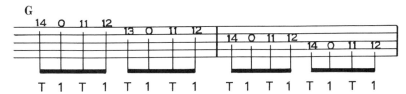

Although the fourth position is quite practical there's a very convenient "half position" which comes in handy for rapid fire bluegrass playing. This is based on the lower three frets of position four.

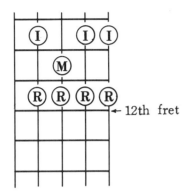

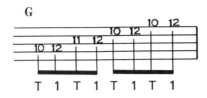

Here's one possibility

which can be expanded to:

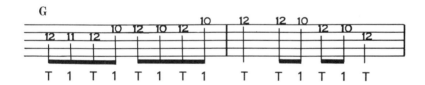

Using these two and an added D-lick, we can come up with an effective single-string version of "Salty Dog."

Salty Dog

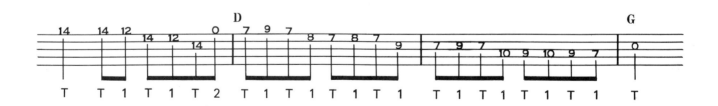

Finish with these.

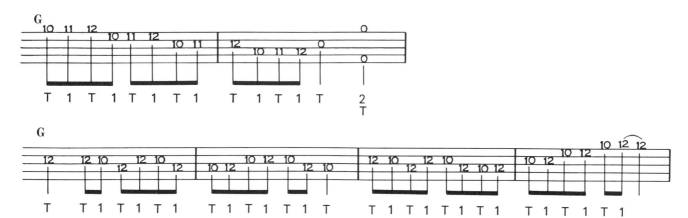

FIFTH POSITION

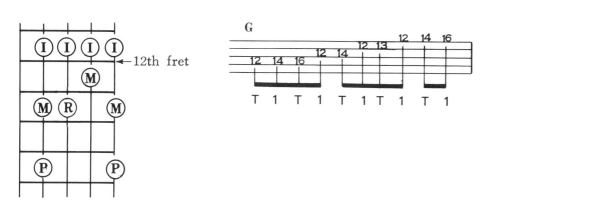

We're going to take a fairly cursory stroll through this position since it's essentially the same as the open-G position taken up an octave. To help your creative flow turn back to the section on open-G licks and see how you can apply them in this position. In the meantime try these.

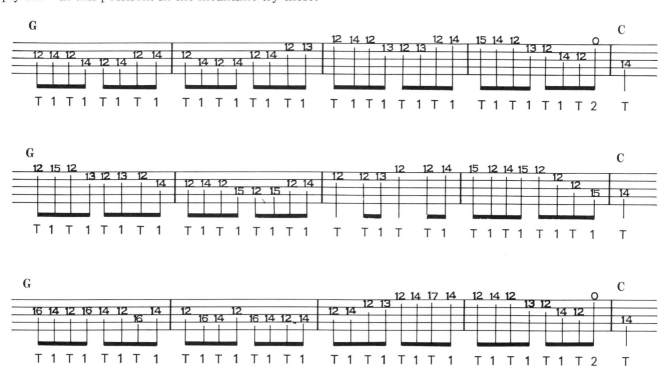

SIXTH POSITION

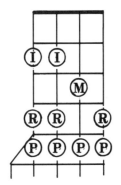

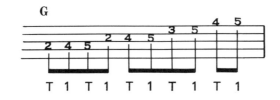

For this position we're moving the whole operation down an octave so we won't have to deal with Munchkin music. Let's start with a lick based on scale patterns.

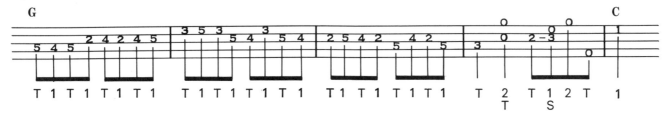

Here's one with an Oriental flavor.

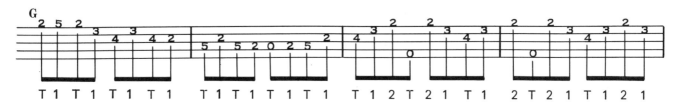

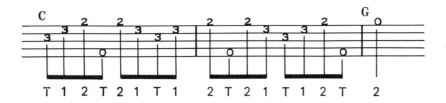

The latter is an expansion of the former.

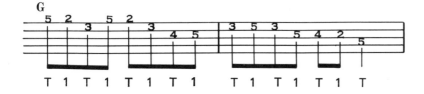

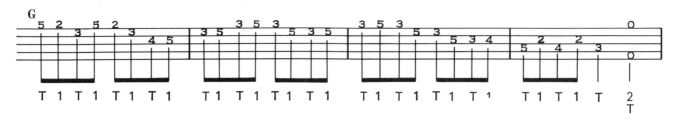

Now, two from the land of chromatics. In terms of the left hand, the first should be played as follows: On the second string alternate the middle and index; on the first string use your index on the 2nd fret, ring on the 3rd and pinky on the 5th.

Chromatic two:

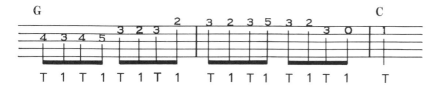

Here's a bluesy lick.

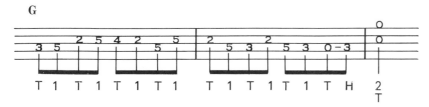

Try the same lick using more open strings.

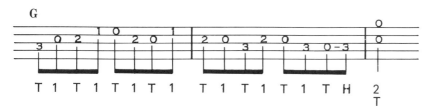

SEVENTH POSITION

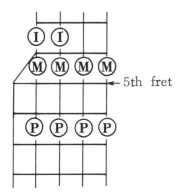

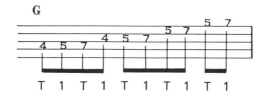

67

This is the last position and for me it's the most comfortable. Sample these.

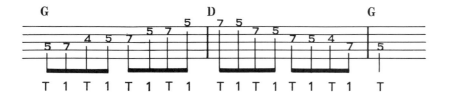

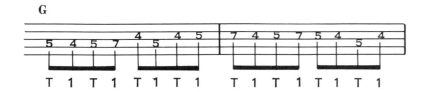

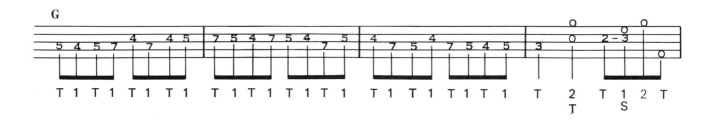

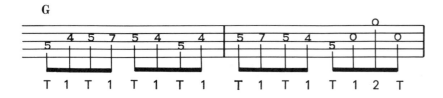

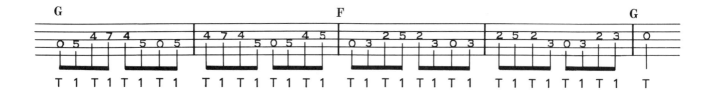

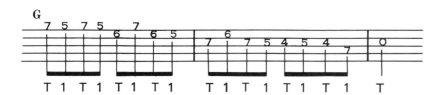

Here's "Black Mountain Rag" to put it all together.

Black Mountain Rag

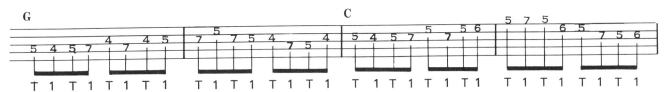

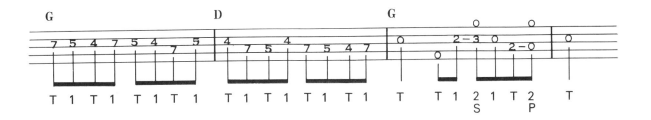

C Licks

I'm going to lay out twenty-one licks for you now, all of which can be played against a C chord. Here's the first batch (second lick courtesy of Peter Elegant, a fine picker from Queens, New York).

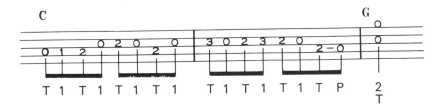

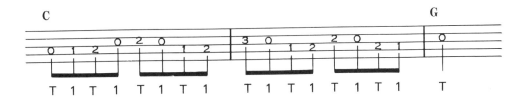

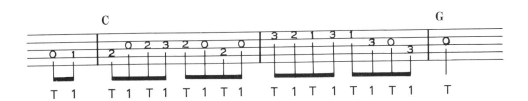

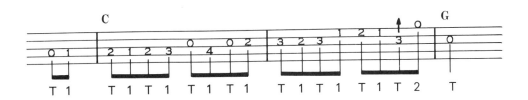

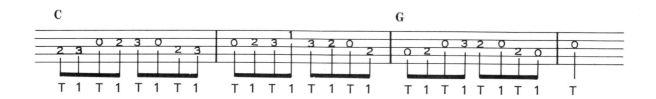

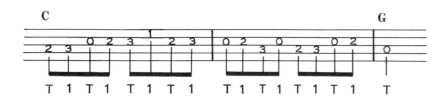

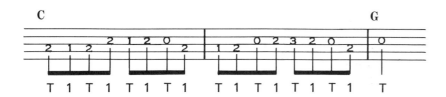

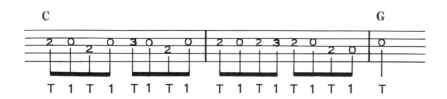

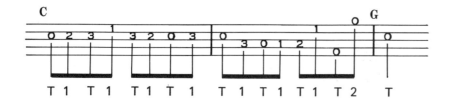

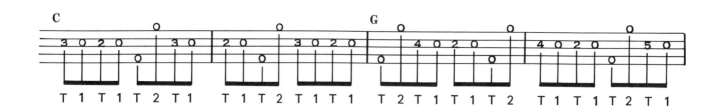

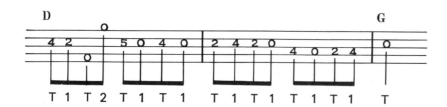

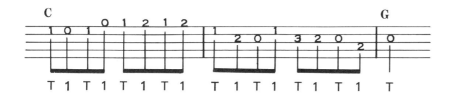

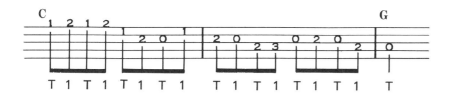

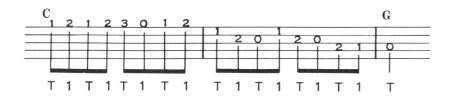

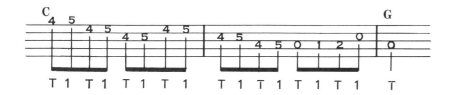

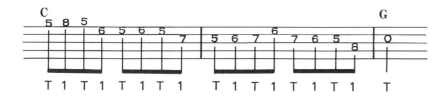

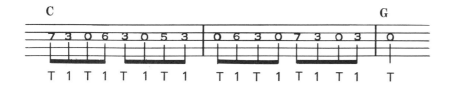

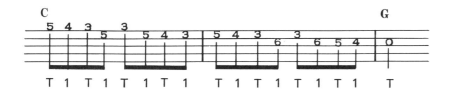

Here are two related licks that fit "John Hardy" to a T.

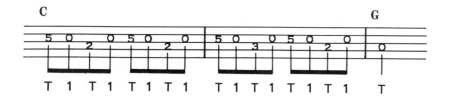

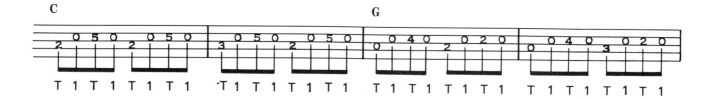

As jazz begins to encroach on bluegrass we find that the convolutions of be-bop are not all that hard to cut on the banjo. Witness these next two C licks. The first has a repetitive motif on the first and fourth strings, nice octave action.

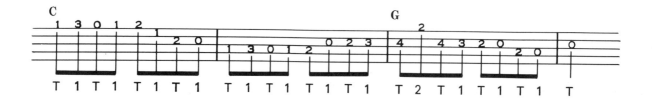

You should begin this lick with the middle finger of your left hand and work from there using one finger per fret. When you get to the third string do the same, this time starting with your index finger.

Here's one for the road from Lauck Benson.

72

D Licks

To round out the I IV V pattern so common to bluegrass here are a collection of D licks.

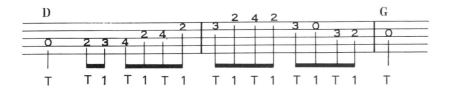

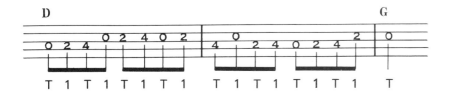

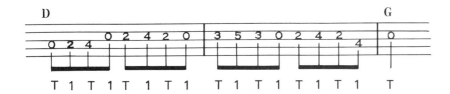

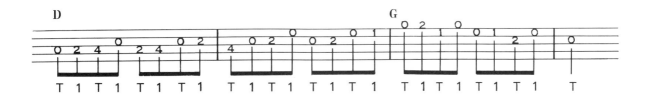

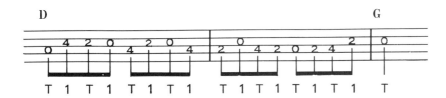

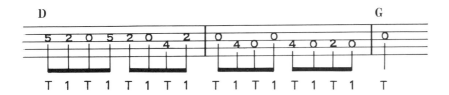

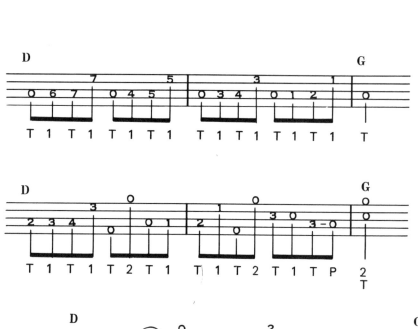

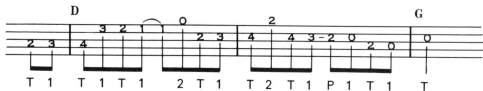

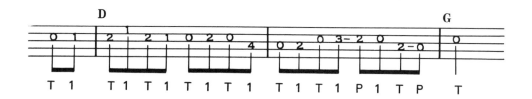

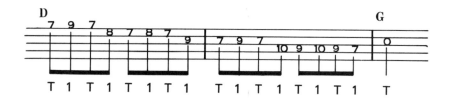

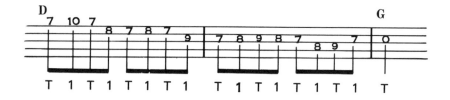

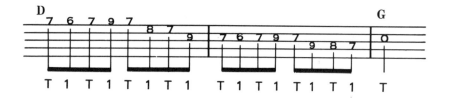

Since we've been dealing with chromatic licks throughout this chapter here are some D offerings. For the first lick, finger with the index, middle, and ring consecutively and then move in jumps from there.

74

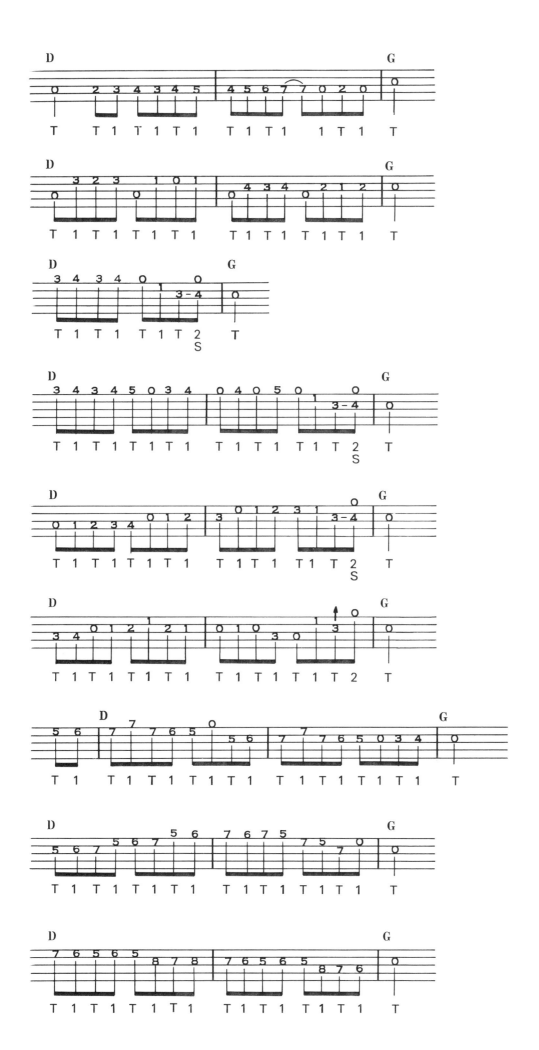

Let's end with an ending.

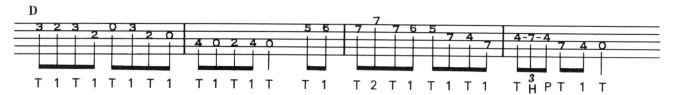

F Licks

F is also a juicy target for the single-string style. You can use the following licks in such tunes as "Little Maggie," "Bluegrass Breakdown," or any other tune that features two measures of F. If you're dealing with just one measure of F, whittle these down to your own specifications. For instance, you could use the following for "Theme Time."

After you work through the following licks, other possibilities will present themselves to you.

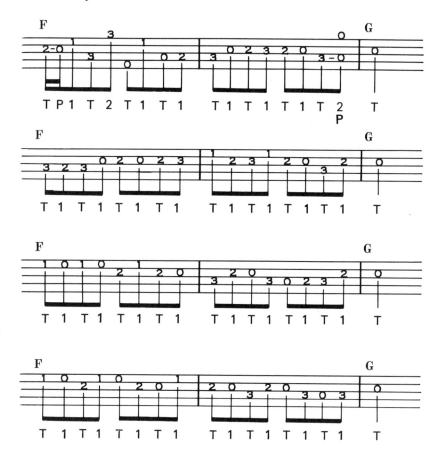

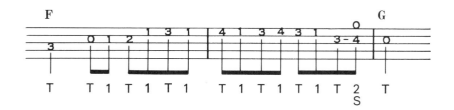

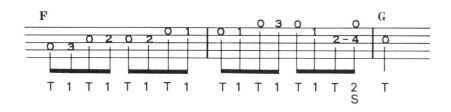

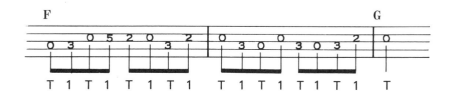

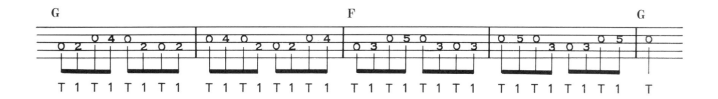

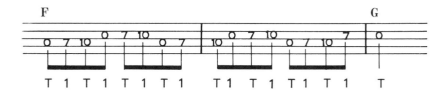

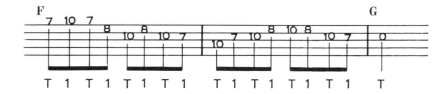

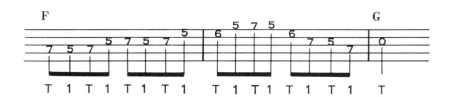

Watch the timing on this last one, and be sure to chop the sustain before the rests.

Here's "Little Maggie" to put this all in context.

Little Maggie

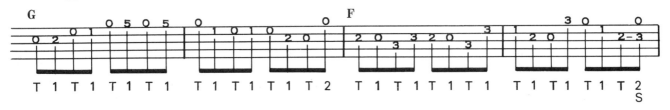

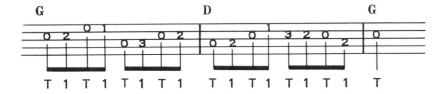

A Licks

Suitable for "Salty Dog" and other songs featuring two measures of A:

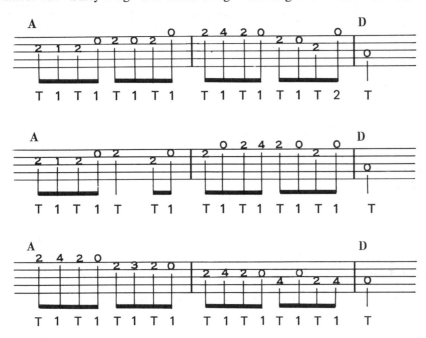

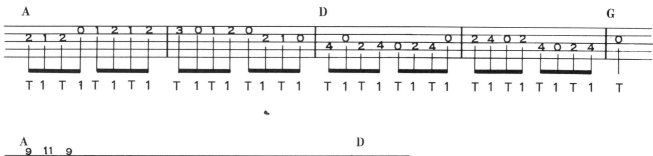

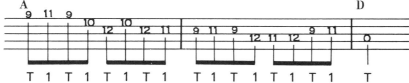

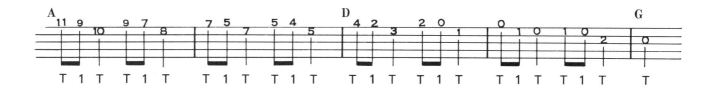

Start this next lick with the middle finger of your left hand and continue on, one finger per fret.

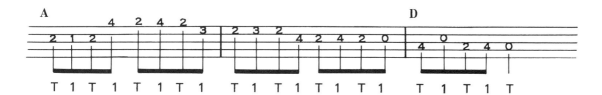

Here are three licks with similar repeating six-note patterns.

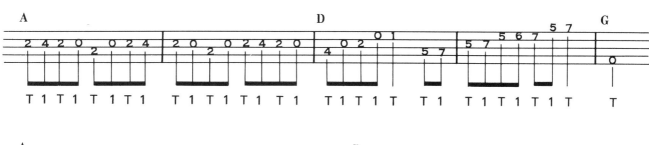

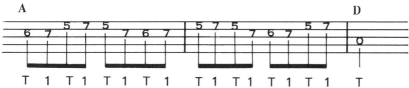

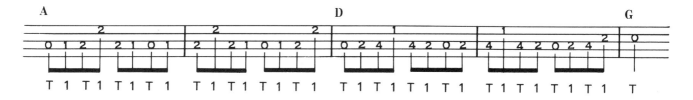

Here's a final bebop lick to tangle with. It's pretty tricky in terms of the left hand, but give it a shot. Start with your middle finger.

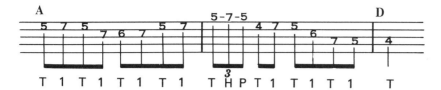

Expanding on Single-String Concepts

One of my favorite musical pastimes involves the expansion of basic motifs. In other words, I'll come up with a lick and then try to find other related permutations. The single-string style seems to be particularly well suited to this activity. For instance, you can take a simple pattern like this

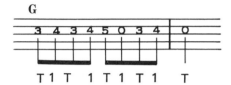

then move it over to the fourth string and complete the thought.

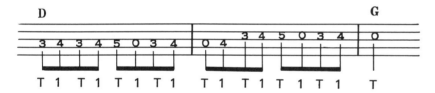

Or you can take the following four notes

then move them down the neck, touching on the notes of a G scale as you go.

Instead of sweeping upward with the four-note riff, we can use a descending motion.

Thus far we've been using strings three and four. Let's move now to the second and third strings.

Here are two related licks.

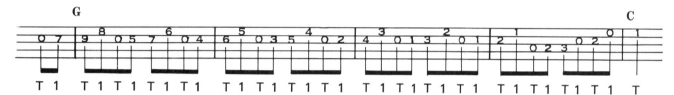

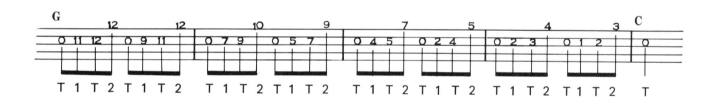

Here's a hot chromatic pattern. First descending:

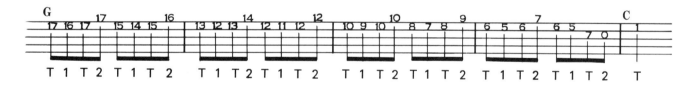

Then ascending:

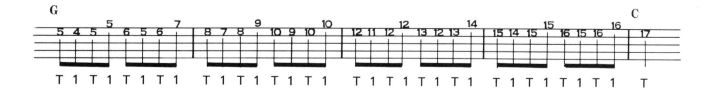

Try it in the context of "John Hardy."

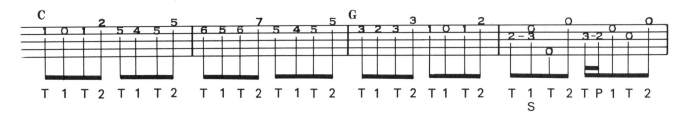

The next four licks are related by the upward or downward chromatic movement of a basic three- or four-note pattern. For the last one, keep your pinky anchored to the second string and your index to the third as you move up and down the neck.

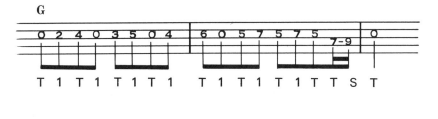

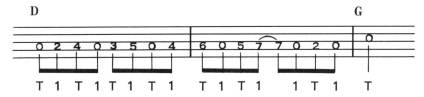

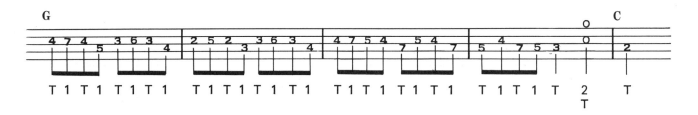

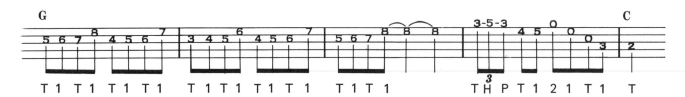

Find the pattern connecting these three chords.

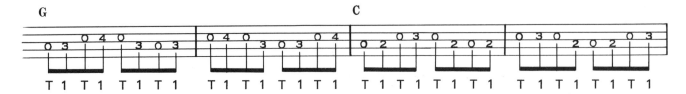

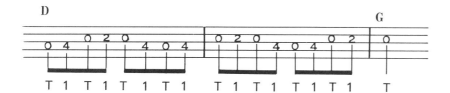

If you can do it on one string you can often do it on another.

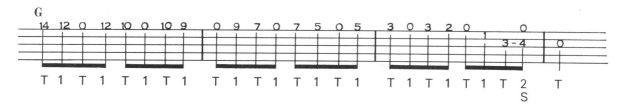

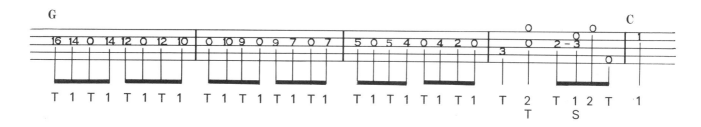

I always think of David Grisman when I work out of this next pattern. It's similar to a riff he uses on the mandolin.

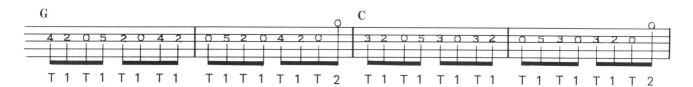

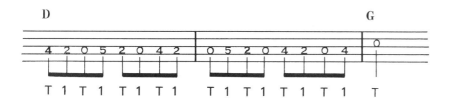

Here it is on two strings.

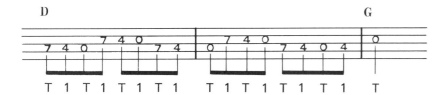

Finish with this memory of Glenn Miller.

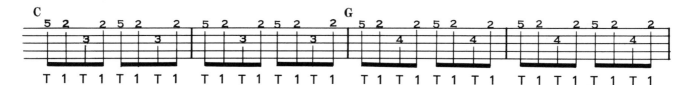

Whole-Tone Passages

A *whole tone* is the distance between two notes which are two half-steps a-part. By stringing a number of them together, you can get some very interest-ing results. Unfortunately, whole-tone passages don't often find their way in-to the bluegrass world because it's in their nature to momentarily obscure the tonal center. Such a lapse can be upsetting for some. But for the stout of heart, press on.

Let's begin with a whole-tone scale moving from G to G on the third string.

Here's a more convenient way of getting the same notes.

Try it starting with a D.

84

Here's G in the closed position.

We can expand the basic whole-tone scale in a number of ways, such as:

and

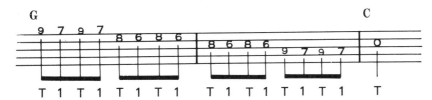

Here's one way to sweep through a D chord.

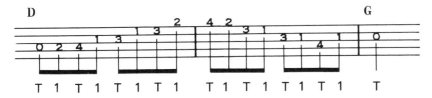

A number of years ago I recorded an album for Rounder Records called *Heartlands*. The opening cut was a somewhat less than traditional rendering of "Roll in My Sweet Baby's Arms." This is a sample of what went on in the opening break. (Whole-tone lick courtesy of Ernest Tubb's Texas Troubadors.)

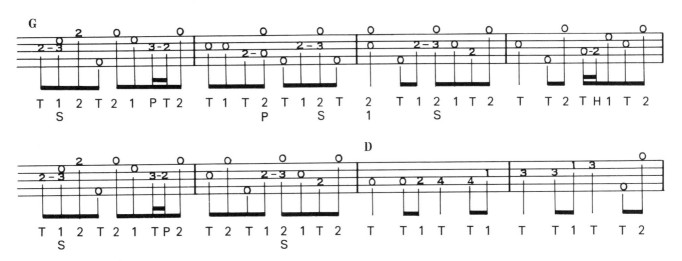

Try this descending whole-tone lick.

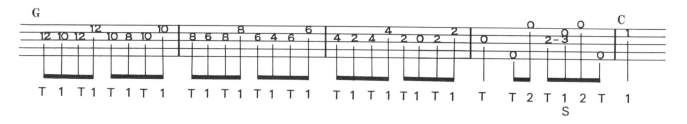

I think this final lick is an appropriate way to close out this section on single-string playing. It's probably the hardest lick we've covered so far and it works as the second half of an ending. Actually it's not really a lick, but rather a two-octave whole-tone scale. Use your index finger for the first two notes and then continue on in the time-honored one-finger-per-fret fashion. Good luck.

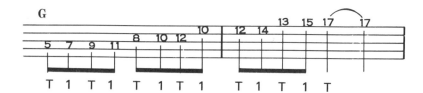

Don Reno and Earl Scruggs in a rare jam at New River Ranch, Rising Sun, Maryland; July 25, 1955

Melodic Style

Having touted the single-string style in the last chapter I'd like to discuss now the virtues of the melodic technique. Bill Keith's name is, of course, inextricably linked to this flowing style and it is almost solely through his efforts that the banjo has been made safe for fiddle tunes. By also creating a wealth of exciting new melodic licks he greatly expanded the improvisatory range of the instrument. Although I won't be including any of his licks per se in this chapter, they do form an hereditary foundation for the ones that follow.

I think most of you have at least a basic understanding of melodic technique, so I'm going to dispense with detailed introductory material. If you do feel the need for a more comprehensive approach I can recommend my first book, *Melodic Banjo* (Oak Publications).

Simply put, the melodic style is based, as is the single-string technique, on scales. Here's the difference, though. Rather than picking one string two or three times in a row, the melodic style requires that you always alternate strings. This means that you are returning, Scruggslike, to the right-hand roll concept absent in single-string technique. The left-hand positions also differ, as this melodic G-scale indicates.

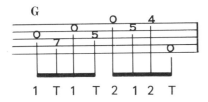

Here's the same scale, extended by one note on either side.

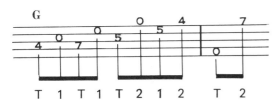

And again, this time flatting the seventh degree of the scale to facilitate movement toward a C chord.

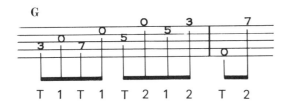

You can also take the G scale partway up the neck to create another area for exploration.

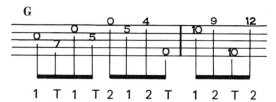

1 T 1 T 2 1 2 T 1 2 T 2

Using these simple scalar positions as a basis you can start working through the following licks.

1 T 1 T 2 1 2 T 1 T 1 T 1 T 1 2 T

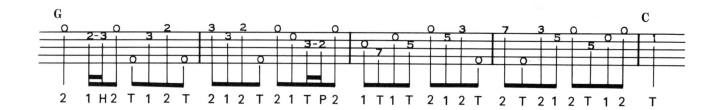

2 1 H 2 T 1 2 T 2 1 2 T 2 1 T P 2 1 T 1 T 2 1 2 T 2 T 2 1 2 T 1 2 T

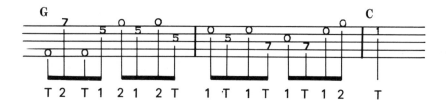

T 2 T 1 2 1 2 T 1 T 1 T 1 T 1 2 T

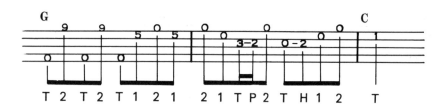

T 2 T 2 T 1 2 1 2 1 T P 2 T H 1 2 T

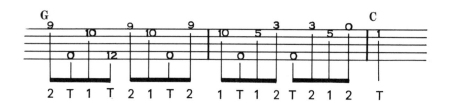

2 T 1 T 2 1 T 2 1 T 1 2 T 2 1 2 T

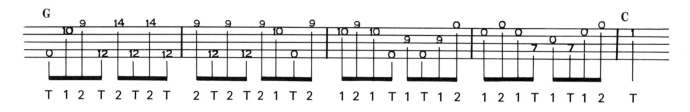

T 1 2 T 2 T 2 T 2 T 2 T 2 1 T 2 1 2 1 T 1 T 1 2 1 2 1 T 1 T 1 2 T

Scale fragments can also be interspersed with Scruggs licks as follows.

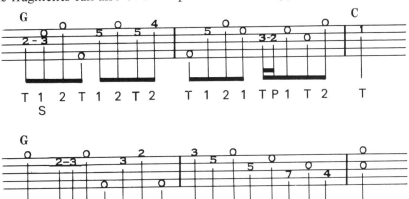

Now try these chromatic variations.

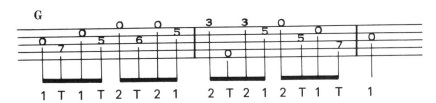

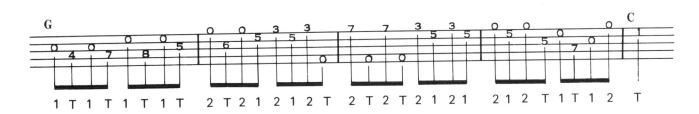

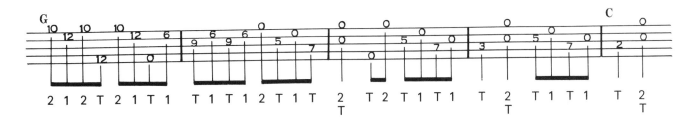

Thus far in this chapter we've been using a loose structure to explain how these licks operate. Now let's tighten things up a bit with a methodical and detailed explanation of melodic lick creation.

Developing Melodic Licks

If you've been playing the banjo for any length of time you're undoubtedly aware of the melodically ascending and descending Keith Thompson licks that have peppered the newgrass idiom for the last ten to fifteen years. In this section I'll also show you how to create an infinite variety of licks based on these theoretical principles.

Let's start by analyzing this ascending lick.

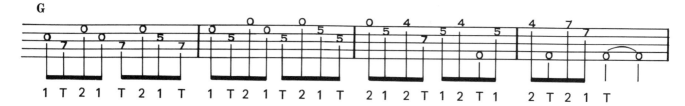

With one quick listening you can sense a certain logic governing the note sequence. Notice first that every note in the lick appears somewhere in the G-major scale (numbers underneath the notes indicate the degree of the scale).

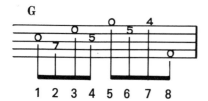

You can see that the first three notes of the lick are the same as the first three notes in the G scale. The fourth note is a repeat of the first note of the scale. So the following pattern has been established in terms of degrees of the scale: 1 2 3 1.

Now look at the next four notes.

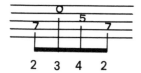

The pattern is the same one found in the first four notes of the lick, this time starting on the second degree of the scale: three consecutively ascending scale notes, dropping back to the initial tone in the series. The third grouping of four notes starts on the third degree of the scale and continues the pattern. If you work through the rest of the lick you'll find that the formula holds true throughout; although in a couple of instances there will be alternate fingerings for certain notes. Here's a practical application.

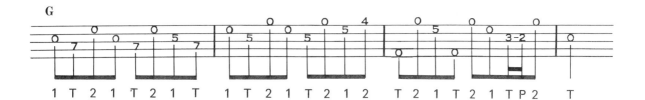

The following is a reverse of the original starting with the fourth note and working backwards, then moving to the eighth note and so forth.

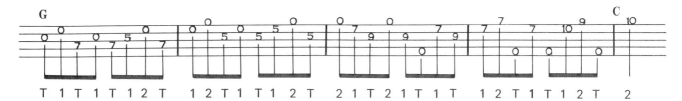

Here's a similar lick.

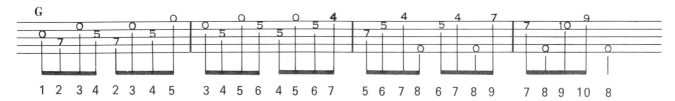

Instead of playing three consecutive notes of the scale and then dropping back to the first note in the sequence, you're playing four consecutive notes, each four-note segment starting with the succeeding degree of the scale. Here's the reverse of this lick, taken in four-note sequences.

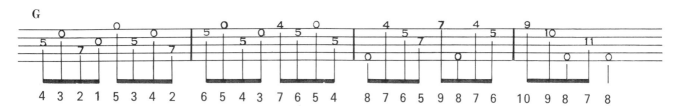

This is the way it could be incorporated into the second half of "Little Maggie."

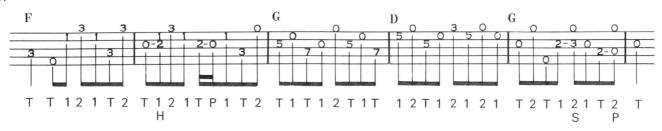

Now let's turn to another pattern. (For future reference remember that the ninth note of the scale is the same as the second taken up an octave, the tenth the same as the third, and so forth.)

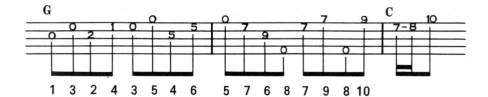

Here we're starting with the first note of the G scale, skipping the second and going on to the third. Then we move to the second degree of the scale, skip one, and arrive at the fourth, continuing on up in two-note sequences. If you start with the first note in the lick and play every other note you'll find yourself playing a G scale.

For a variation, try skipping two notes of the scale at a time.

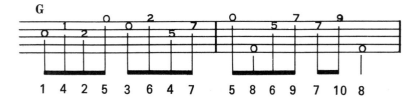

You're working again in a two-note sequence, starting with the first note of the scale, skipping the second and third notes and playing the fourth. Then you go to the second note of the scale, skipping the third and fourth and playing the fifth, and so on.

Here's a variation on a theme and its adaptation to lick form.

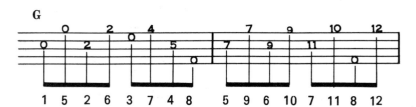

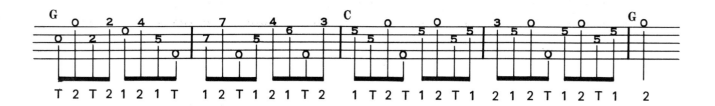

Try these ascending patterns.

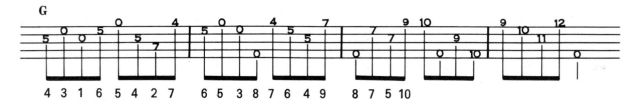

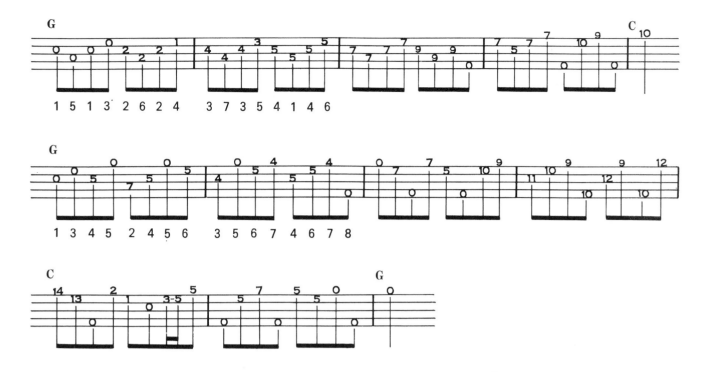

You can also get some nice chromatic effects by systematically flatting each
note of the scale as follows.

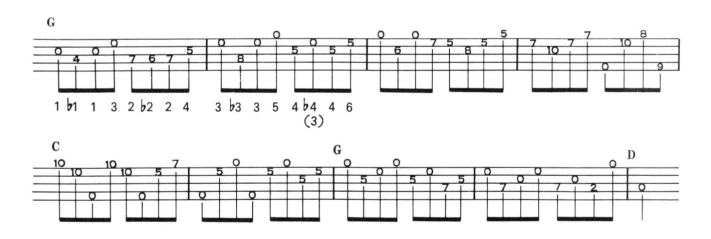

Of course, you don't always have to ascend, you can descend as well. Here's
a very familiar lick with its note sequence explained.

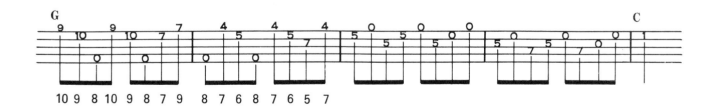

You can also start on the eighth note of the lick and excerpt a ready-made D pattern.

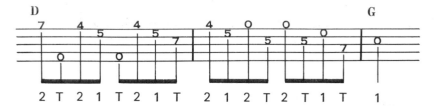

I'd like to end this section by giving you a little work to do. Determine the pattern operating in these next two licks.

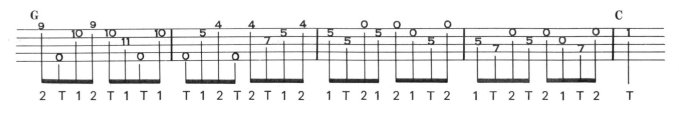

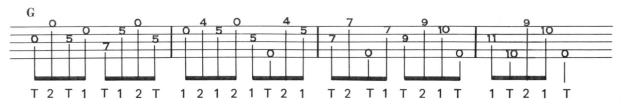

G-LICK POSTLUDE

Here are a few last scattered G licks I'd like to throw your way.

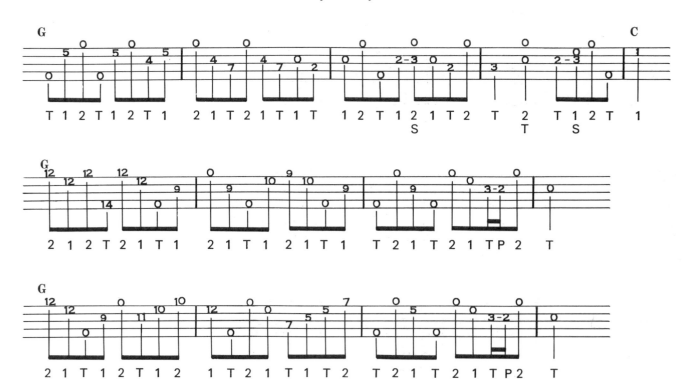

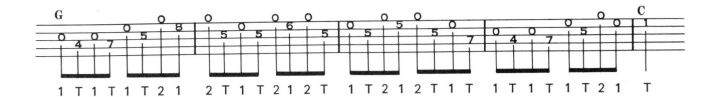

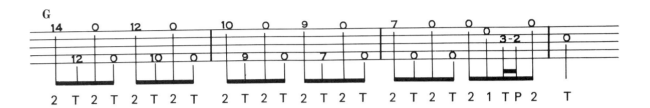

C Licks

Since there is only one note difference between a C and G scale (an F instead of an F♯) you'll have no trouble playing a melodic C-scale.

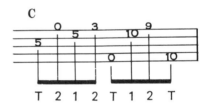

With some help from the single-string department we can extend the lower range of the C scale down to a D note.

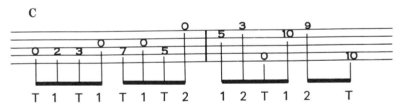

With this information at your fingertips we can construct a series of C licks, each one based on a different note of the scale. Let's begin at the bottom with the open D-string, the second note of the C scale. This first lick is based on a C *pentatonic scale*; in other words, a five-note scale encompassing the first, second, third, fifth, and sixth scale-tones in C. (Numbers at the bottom indicate the degrees of the scale.)

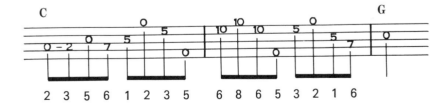

Starting with the third note of the C scale (E) we have these two possibilities. (Notice the pentatonic character of the second lick.)

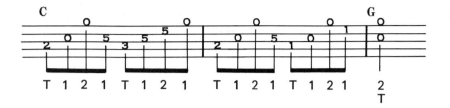

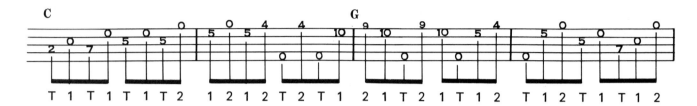

Here's another, starting on E. It's not all that practical for inclusion in fiery bluegrass standards but its quiet peace can be enjoyed at a slow tempo.

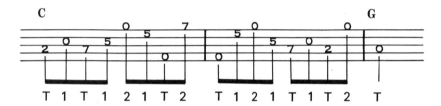

Practice your broken-field playing on this one starting on the fourth note of the C scale.

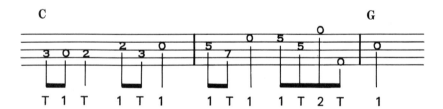

Two from five. For the second, try to keep your pinky planted on the fourth string, 7th fret.

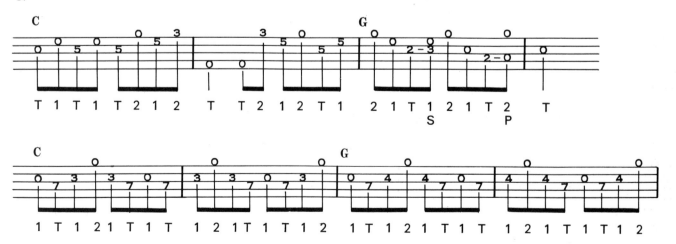

Leaving from six:

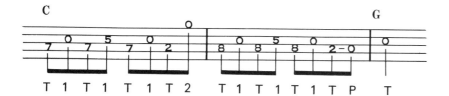

This one starts on the flatted-seventh note of the scale and should keep your left hand scurrying.

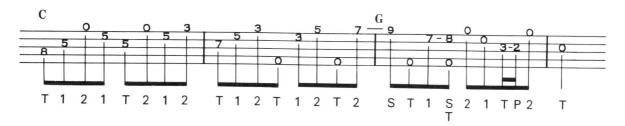

Now the major seventh:

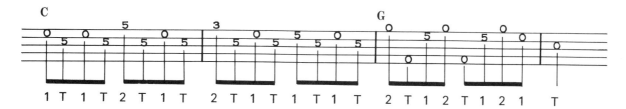

Finally we return to the first, or eighth tone of the C scale.

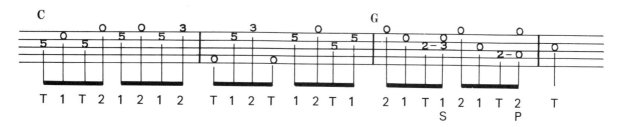

Now try this assortment.

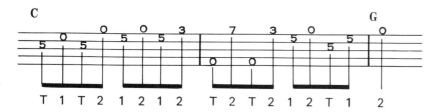

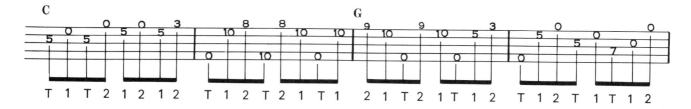

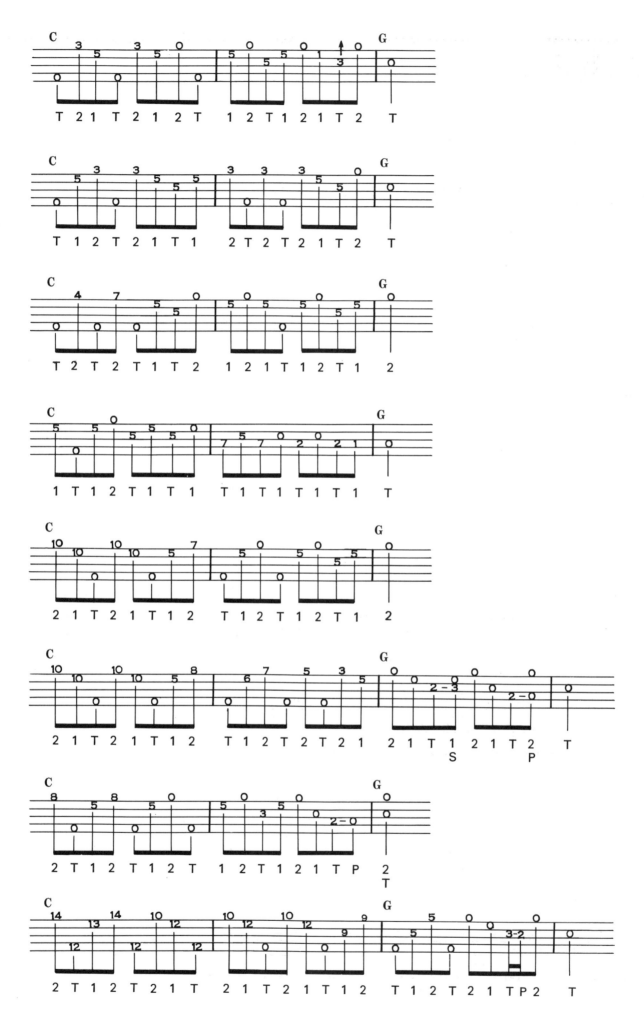

D Licks

Start with this two-octave D scale.

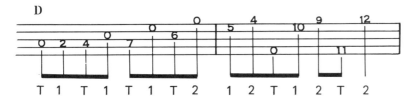

By flatting the seventh degree of the scale (C♯) one half-step (to C) your licks will be much more compatible in the key of G. In fact, in changing the C♯ to a C, the D scale becomes a G scale starting on a D note.

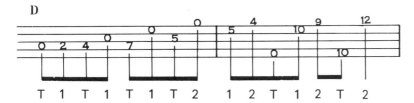

To give you more of a feel for what's going on here, try this long-winded exercise.

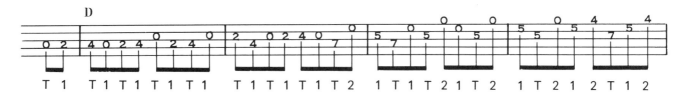

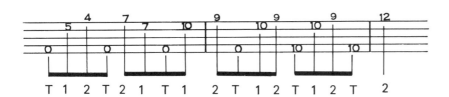

As in the C section I've based the following licks on successive notes of the scale (in this case D). See if you can do the same. You'll find that it makes a great exercise for stretching your creativity.

Start on 1

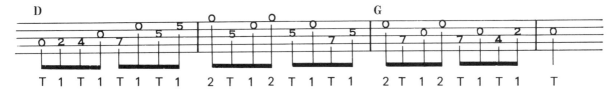

99

Start on 2

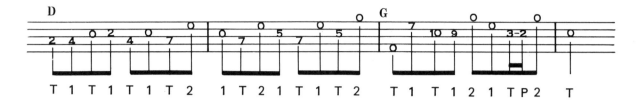

T 1 T 1 T 1 T 2   1 T 2 1 T 1 T 2   T 1 T 1 2 1 T P 2   T

Start on 3

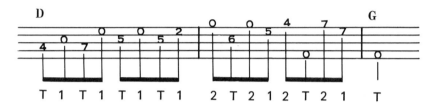

T 1 T 1 T 1 T 1   2 T 2 1 2 T 2 1   T

Start on 4

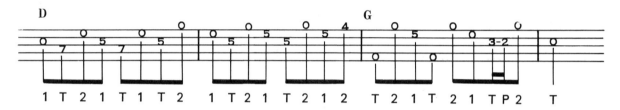

1 T 2 1 T 1 T 2   1 T 2 1 T 2 1 2   T 2 1 T 2 1 T P 2   T

Start on 5

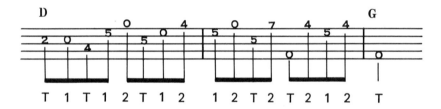

T 1 T 1 2 T 1 2   1 2 T 2 T 2 1 2   T

Start on 6

1 T 2 1 T 2 1 T   1 T 2 1 T 1 T 1   T

Start on flat-7

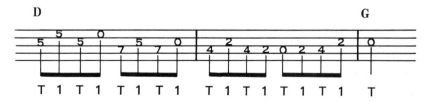

T 1 T 1 T 1 T 1   T 1 T 1 T 1 T 1   T

Start on 8

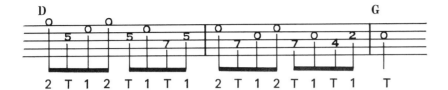

Here's a sampling of melodic D-licks, suitable for all non-trad occasions.

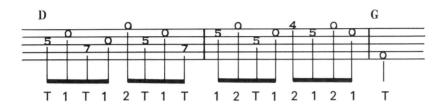

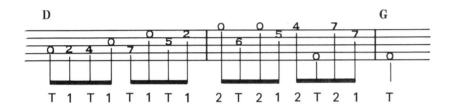

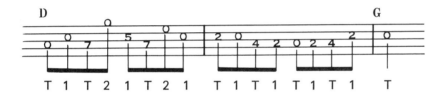

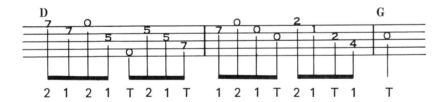

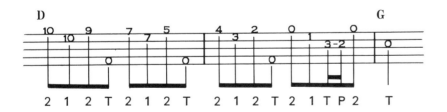

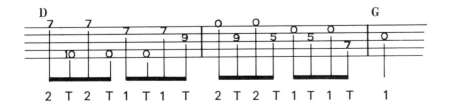

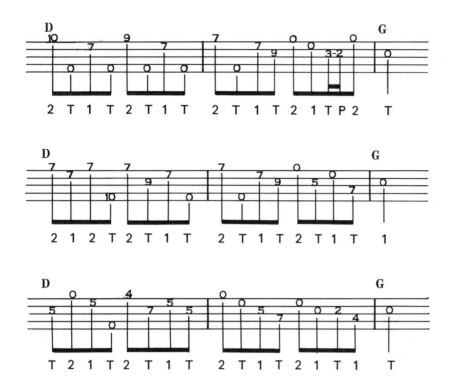

An A diminished chord, and it's accompanying family, makes a good D substitute. With that thought in mind, here are the last two offerings in this section.

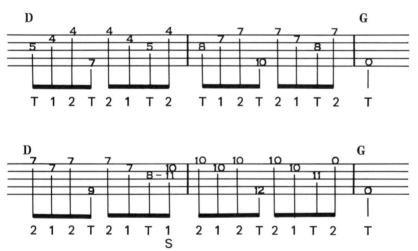

F Licks

F makes a good chordal base for melodics. In other words, you'll find that chord tones alternating with open strings give the most fluid results. There'll be less reliance on the F scale per se. For instance:

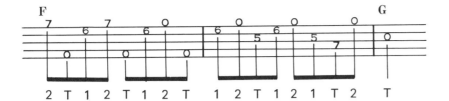

What scale action there is tends to be of a more pentatonic nature (as in the above lick). As I mentioned earlier, a pentatonic scale consists of five notes, in this case, the first, second, third, fifth, and sixth degrees. Here are two examples an octave apart.

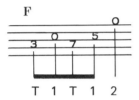 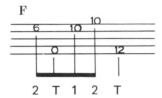

Their extension:

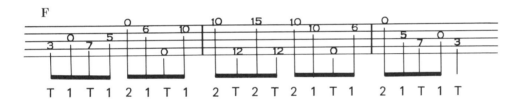

Try these practical applications.

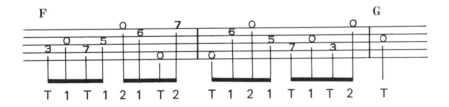

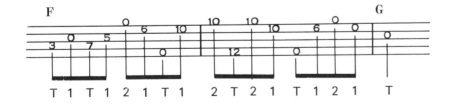

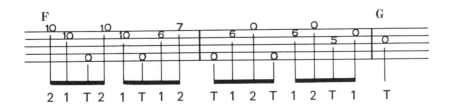

The following are not strictly pentatonic, but include blues and chromatic tones to achieve their effect.

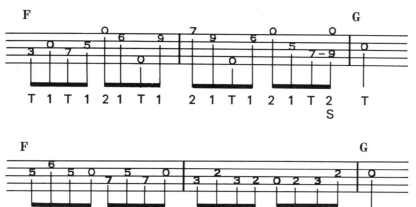

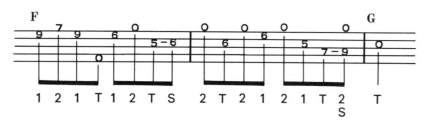

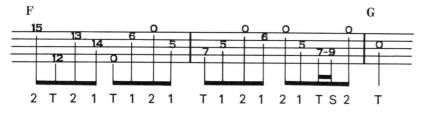

Here's "Little Maggie" for context.

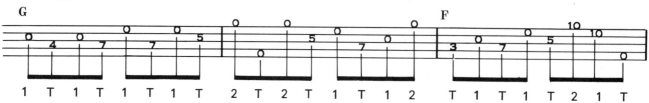

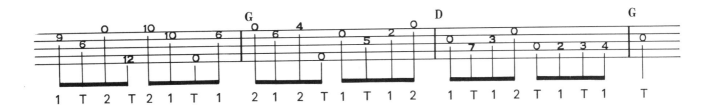

A Licks

As was the case with F, many A licks can be derived directly from the 7th-fret position. For instance:

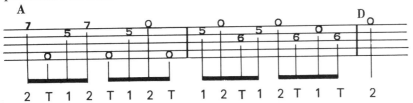

The melodic A-scale also comes from this vicinity.

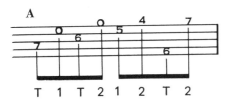

To fit more closely with the D and G tonalities we flat the seventh note of the scale thusly.

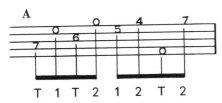

This then becomes a D scale starting on the fifth note of that scale.

With the exception of the last three licks in this section, you'll be working with two measures of A. In terms of practical application, "Salty Dog" is the tune which comes immediately to mind.

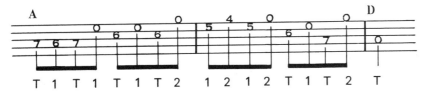

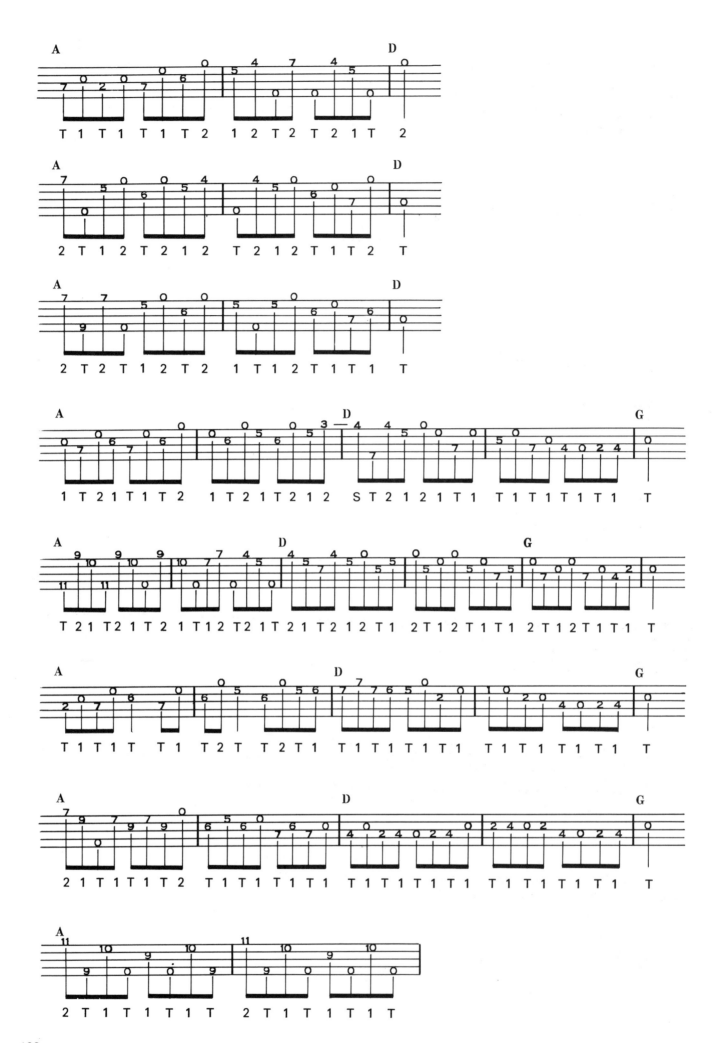

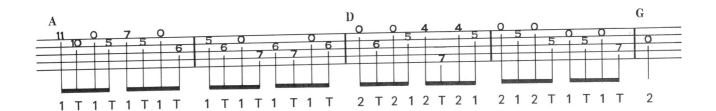

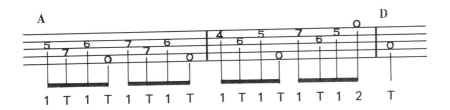

Here are three single measure shots.

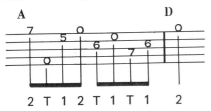

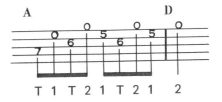

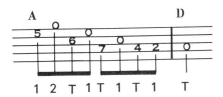

Blues Licks

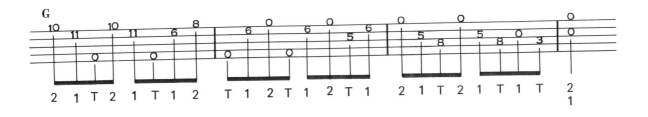

Sound familiar? It should. It's the prototypical melodically descending blues lick loved and played by millions. But where does it come from? Let's check in with a B♭ scale to start our investigation.

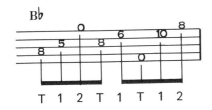

If we excerpt the first, second, third, fifth, sixth, and eighth notes of that scale we come up with the following pentatonic concoction.

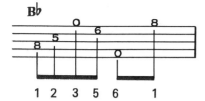

This becomes the basis for all melodic blues-licks in G. For perspective, start on a G note.

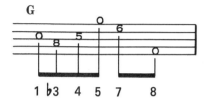

In the context of this G scale you now have the one, flat-three, four, five, flat-seven, and eight. Here it is stretched out.

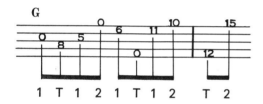

The G licks that follow are based on the abovementioned notes although strict adherence is not maintained.

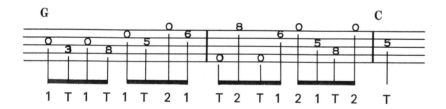

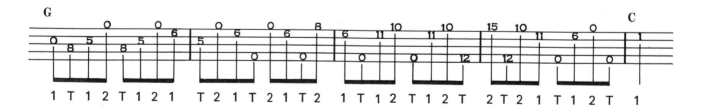

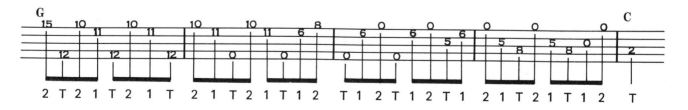

108

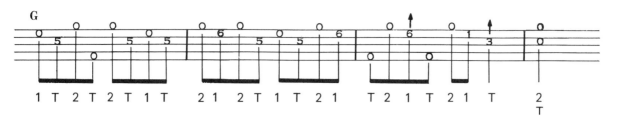

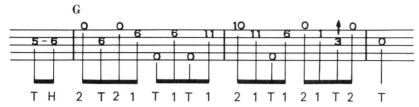

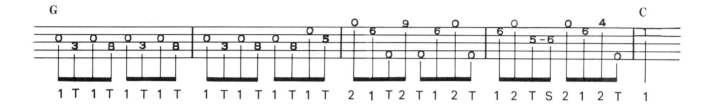

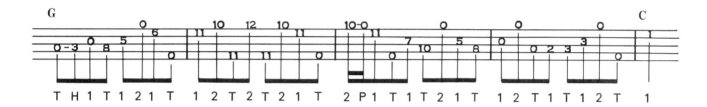

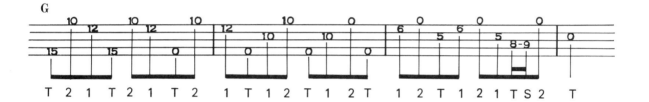

You can also apply the notes in a G blues-scale to C.

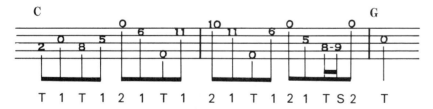

Here are some more examples.

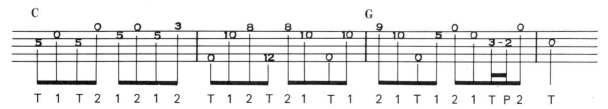

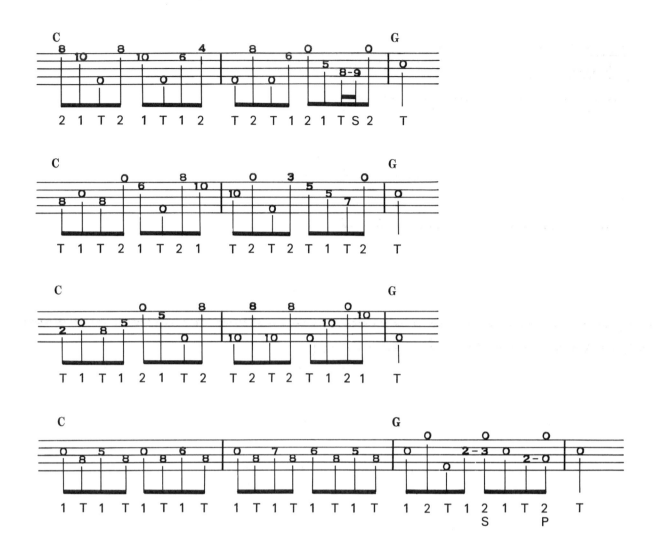

For D blues-licks, take the one, flat-three, four, five, and flat-seven out of a D scale.

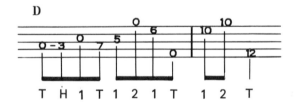

That will give you the foundation for the following licks.

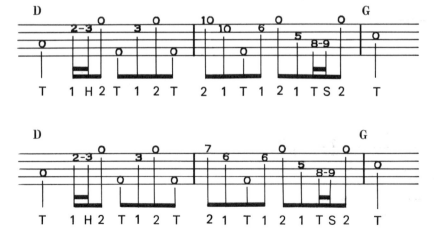

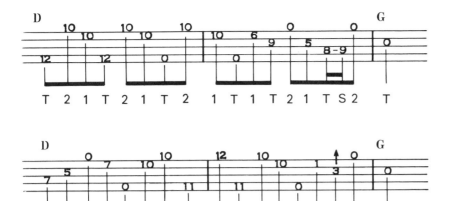

Chromatic Licks

We've been using chromatic intervals all the way through this book, but so far we haven't discussed them in detail. So . . .

Chromatic notes are neighboring notes which are one half-step (one fret) apart. To get these notes you'll find yourself looking beyond the standard diatonic (*do re mi*) scale to the additional spaces between. Here's a one-octave chromatic G-scale to illustrate.

That's a very linear representation. Now try this melodic version of the same scale.

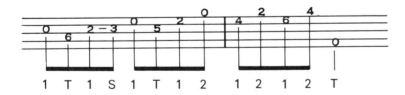

Here it is extended up to B and D.

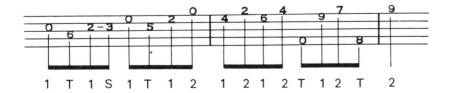

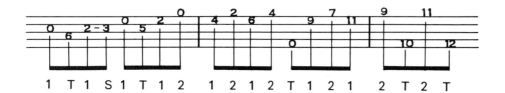

1 T 1 S 1 T 1 2   1 2 1 2 T 1 2 1   2 T 2 T

I've never heard Ben Eldridge pick this next lick but to me it characterizes one aspect of his style (suitable for "I Wonder Where You Are Tonight").

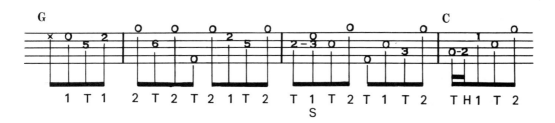

1 T 1   2 T 2 T 2 1 T 2   T 1 T 2 T 1 T 2   T H 1 T 2
                            S

Have some more.

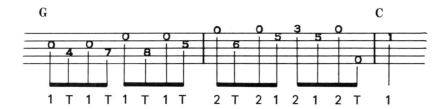

1 T 1 T 1 T 1 T   2 T 2 1 2 1 2 T   1

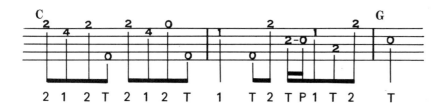

2 1 2 T 2 1 2 T   1   T 2 T P 1 T 2   T

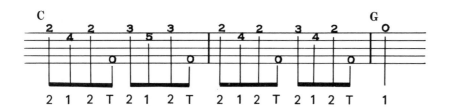

2 1 2 T 2 1 2 T   2 1 2 T 2 1 2 T   1

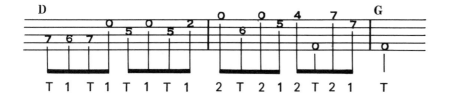

T 1 T 1 T 1 T 1   2 T 2 1 2 T 2 1   T

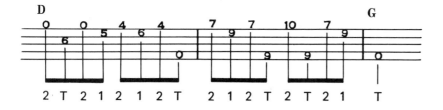

2 T 2 1 2 1 2 T   2 1 2 T 2 T 2 1   T

112

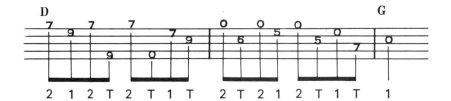

Here's a handy left-hand position to give you some fast chromatics.

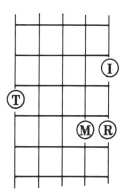

For example:

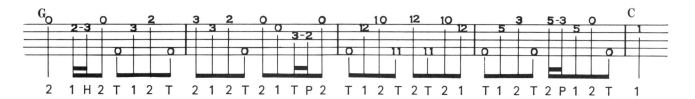

Here are four more based on the same position.

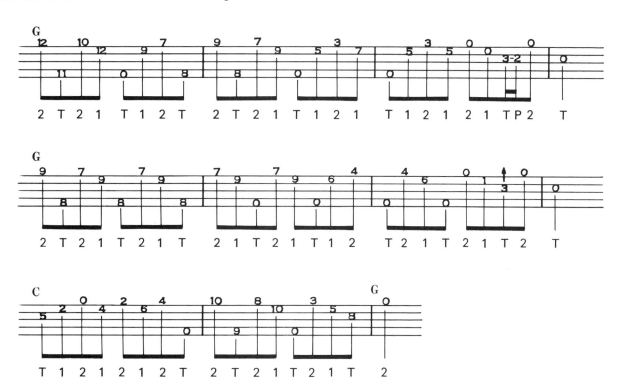

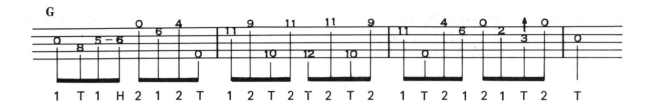

Some other possibilities (with thanks to Marty Cutler for the first).

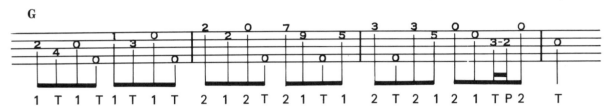

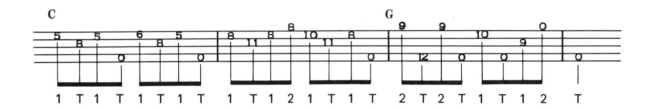

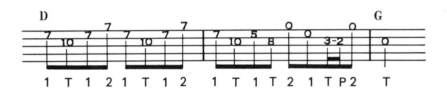

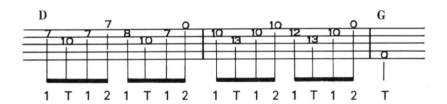

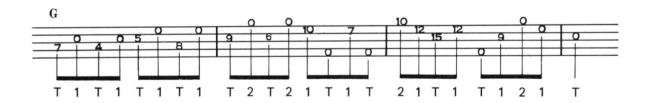

This last lick is ambiguous enough to fit into any chordal situation. Start anywhere on the neck and work your way up from there. (Commonly known as B.S.)

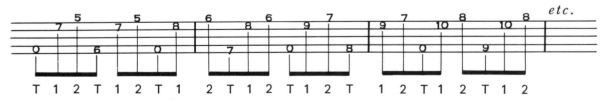

114

Tritone Licks

If two notes are separated by three whole-steps (six half-steps) the interval between them is called a *tritone*. In other words you can fret the third string at the 3rd fret, then move up to the 9th fret. That interval is a tritone. For the sake of practicality you should take the high note (E) and move it over to the second string.

This implies the tonality of a C7, with the third-string note (B♭) being the flatted-seventh note of a C scale and the second-string note (E) being the third note of a C scale. Here are two more C tritones in the same vicinity, this time with the third note of the scale on the bottom and the flatted-seventh on top.

If we chart these three positions out on the fingerboard we get the following.

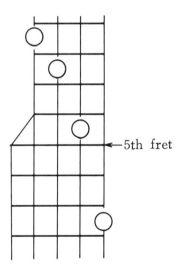

←—5th fret

If you play any two adjoining strings, you'll get a tritone. The interesting thing about all this is the fact that you can move the whole procedure up one fret to create G tritones. In this case the position of sevenths and thirds in the intervals will be the reverse of C. Taking it one step further you can move up one more fret to get D tritones. Also you can take any one of these positions and move it six frets up the neck to create a tritone (also with scale degrees reversed) that will fit against the same chord you were using for the lower position. But enough talk. Here are four exercises out of which you should be able to spin a whole catalogue of licks.

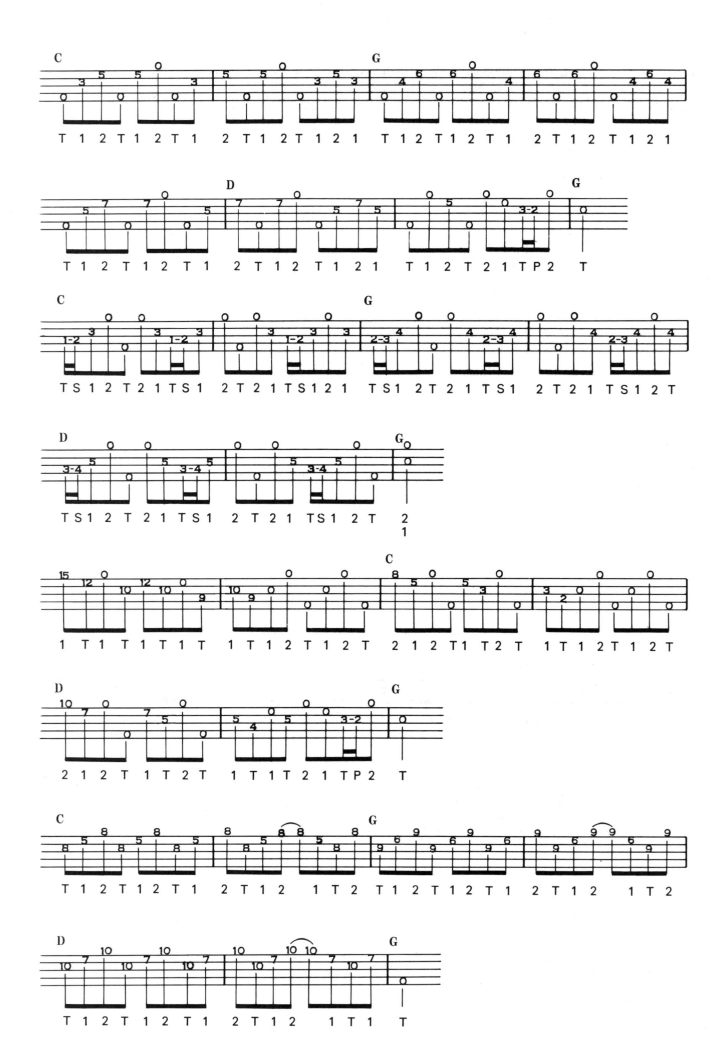

Licks with Diverging Lines

I think you'll have a lot of fun with this next section. It features licks which have two musical lines going in opposite directions. Make sure to use the right side of your brain for the ascending line and the left side for descending. Keeping that in mind, so to speak, check this first kickoff lick which, I believe, comes from the playing of Bill Keith.

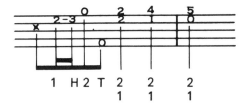

Here's a close relative.

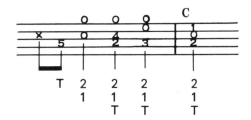

Next, a diverging D-exercise with accompanying lick, also from the fertile imagination of Mr. Keith.

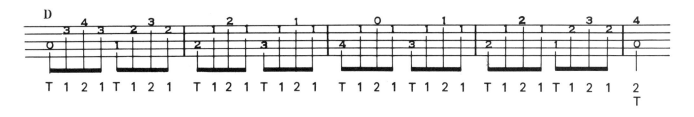

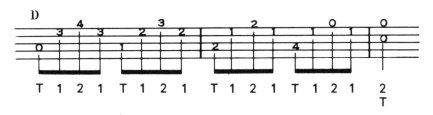

Try this short snippet.

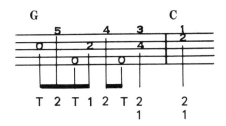

The next two can be connected if desired.

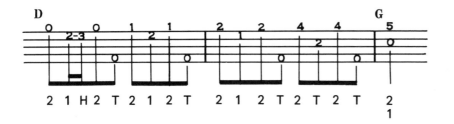

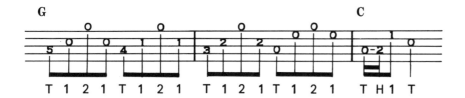

The rise and fall of a D13.

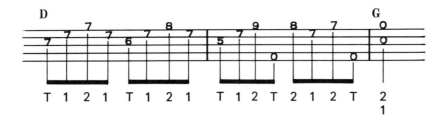

Two for F: In the second lick, fret the 1st fret, fourth string with the thumb of your left hand.

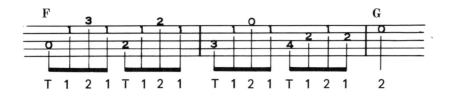

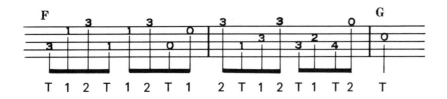

118

This is my Aaron Copland impression.

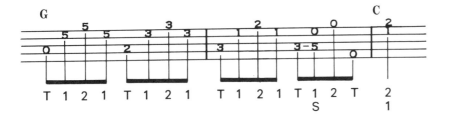

Finally, in C:

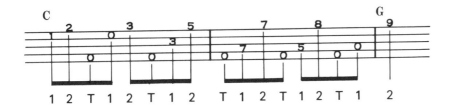

Celebrity Section

In this section we'll be listening to some other voices. Participants include J.D Crowe, Don Reno, Bill Keith, Alan Munde, Peter Wernick, Bela Fleck, Marty Cutler, Peter Schwimmer, and Dave Griffith. You may notice that the scales here tip to the modern end of the spectrum. My intention in arranging things this way is to give you a sense for the limitless reaches of the banjo. You see, there's a lot more going on with that fingerboard than you might imagine. Still, you should remember that even with the most experimental of these players, their home reference point remains forever Scruggs style. You can't speak with authority from the "outside" until you've mastered the ground rules.

J.D. Crowe

A product of Jimmy Martin's glory years, J.D Crowe learned his lessons well. The thing that knocks me out about J.D.'s playing is the ingenious way he has of recombining the elements of Scruggs style. The third lick down is a perfect example; absolutely straight ahead and yet totally original. Just when you thought there was nothing new to say in the traditional style, Zap! there's J.D.

Just a word about this last lick. It's an ending, and it looks easy, but watch out for those chokes. Remember, the ascending arrow connected to the descending arrow means that you should choke up, hold the choke, and then release it.

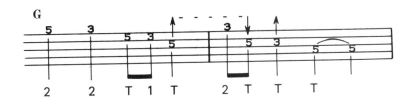

Don Reno

In many ways Don Reno is the most wildly inventive banjo player to ever hit the bluegrass world. In the late forties he made the decision to spice up his traditional style with a more jazz-oriented approach. To do this he developed the single-string style, added cascades of triplets, thumb-led downstrokes, and a knowledge of the guitar fingerboard, put them all together and created an exotic body of licks which few have dared to emulate.

This first lick bears out the notion that Don was the world's first true rock 'n' roll banjo player.

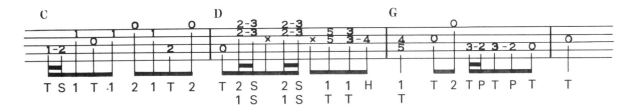

This next lick, with its flurry of triplets should only be attempted in slow to medium tunes. This is one of my favorites.

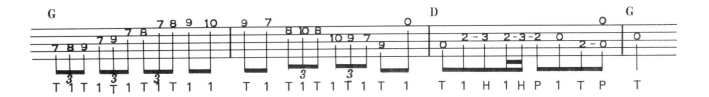

Try these two single-stringers.

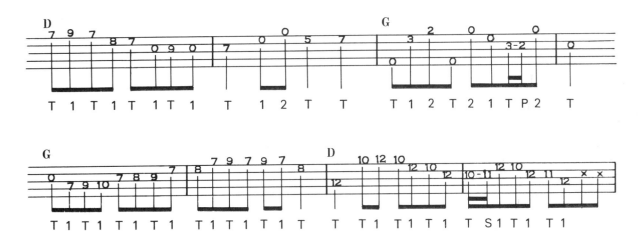

We finish with a ferocious D-lick.

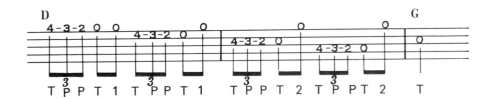

Bill Keith

I think I've said enough about Bill Keith to fill several books. His inestimable contributions to the banjo are well known. His sense of humor on and off the banjo is also not to be underestimated. (See last lick.)

The first four licks exemplify the logic which Bill brings to his music. I think it's this quality which has made his playing so influential. Lick number one is a reworking of the old standard, "Pretty Baby." Use your ring finger and pinky for the first two notes and fret the fourth note with your index.

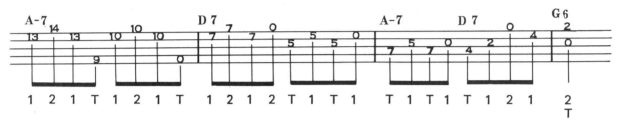

The next two are not really applicable in a bluegrass sense but they make fascinating chordal exercises. The two are almost identical, just transposed into different keys.

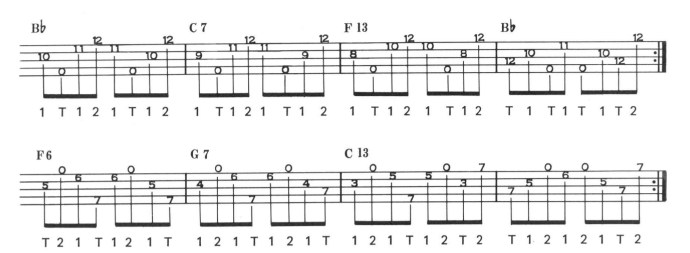

Lick number four, according to Bill, is reminiscent of Paganini's "Perpetual Motion." To my ears it also has somewhat of a bebop ring to it.

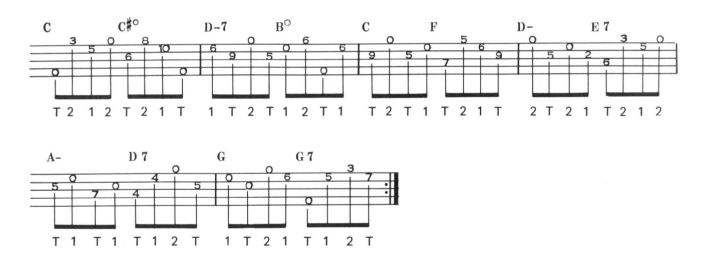

Bill says of this last one, "When beyond all help, try this and sing along."

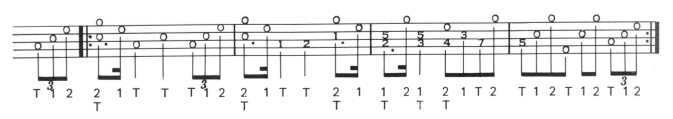

Alan Munde

Alan is also an alumni of Jimmy Martin's Sunny Mountain Boys which undoubtedly accounts for his incredible drive. Credit for his wide-reaching imagination and general banjo role-stretching resides primarily within himself. A long-term member in good standing of Country Gazette, Alan is truly the banjo player's banjo player. His comments follow.

"This is a nice little phrase for moving from D-minor to G7 to C. I use it in a tune that fellow Gazetter Joe Carr and I wrote. Seems I've heard some jazz players play a similar line.

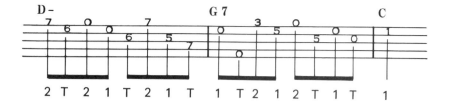

"I learned this descending passage from banjo picker Kenny Ingram, formerly with Jimmy Martin and Lester Flatt. I used it on the Country Gazette recording of 'Hot Burrito Breakdown' from the album *Traitor in Our Midst.*

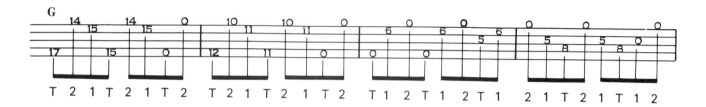

"Pulloffs are among my favorite things to do and this particular lick has a few. Check out 'Deputy Dalton' by Country Gazette on *Don't Give up Your Day Job.*

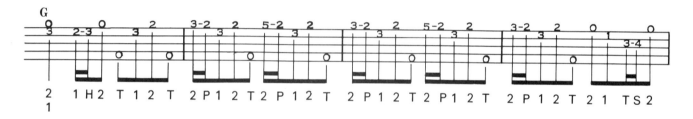

"I use this in 'Dear Old Dixie' on *Alan Munde's Banjo Sandwich* to move through an A7 chord to D.

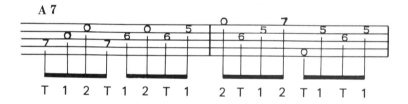

"This lick forms the basis for the chorus of 'The Earl of Broadfield' on *The Banjo Kid Picks Again.*"

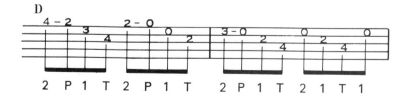

Peter Wernick

Ole Doc Banjo and myself go back a long way, even before Country Cooking when we were referring to ourselves as The Contraband Countryband. Since those days in the early seventies Peter has become the paterfamilias of the banjo world. His book *Bluegrass Banjo* (Oak Publications) is now a world-wide bestseller and for good reason. Peter has the ability to translate even the most difficult concepts into down-to-earth terms. And his playing: It's a joy to hear him pick because it's obvious that he loves to do it. And that's a contagious feeling. Eschewing flash in favor of what works best in a given situation, Peter is a rock-solid interpreter of the past, present, and future. Catch him with Hot Rize. Now over to you, Peter.

"The first two licks are based on relatively easy rolls, so their 'hotness' is not based in their difficulty but rather in the ease with which you can put some force behind them. I find that if a lick requires unnatural movements, I'm less likely to play it with good timing, touch, and tone. So I tend to favor moves I find easier, for more comfort and enjoyable grooving.

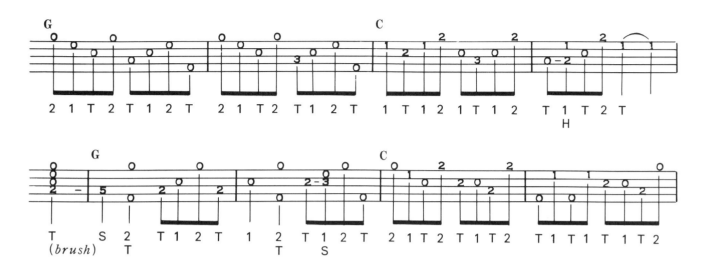

"The next three licks are, on the other hand, not especially natural, but I worked them up to have some of my own touches to use in the forceful, medium-tempo style known in Hot Rize as 'the New York rhythm.'

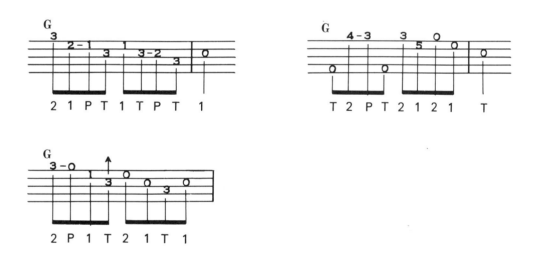

"This last lick is a melodic combination of notes from G and C7 chords, which can be used against these or any other chord in Western music, depending on how deviant you choose to be."

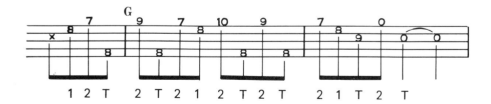

Bela Fleck

In a remarkably short time Bela Fleck has risen to the highest echelons of banjodom (without the aid of a net). This is a tribute to his mind-boggling technique, wide-ranging imagination, and authentic control of both the Scruggs and jazz idioms.

Born and raised in New York City, Bela moved to Boston to hold down the banjo chair with Tasty Licks. In time their experimental forays gave way to tradgrass with the departure of Stacy Phillips on dobro and the addition of Pat Enright on guitar. Appropriate stylistic changes ensued and soon Bela was primed for a move to Lexington, Kentucky. There he helped to form Spectrum, bought two old Mastertones, and traded his Yankee right hand for a Southern.

Here's what Sonny Osborne has to say about Bela: "This young man, if he keeps his head in the direction he's going, is destined to become one of the real greats."

Now before I lay out Bela's five licks I should mention that the first lick comes from "Blue Days, Black Nights" on Tasty Licks' second Rounder album. The fourth lick, a nice jazz turn, can be heard in the midst of "How Can You Face Me Now" from Bela's first solo record, *Crossing the Tracks*, also on Rounder.

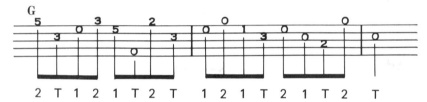

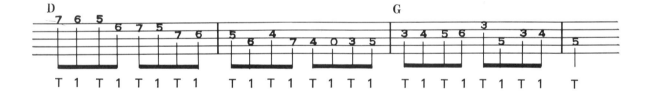

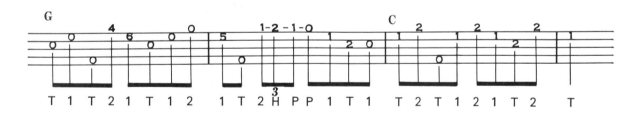

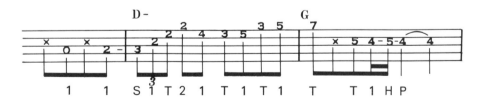

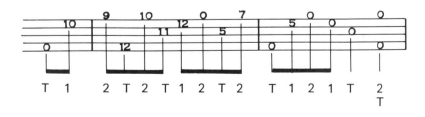

Marty Cutler

Marty Cutler is an ardent lover of iguanas. He also happens to love the banjo. Be it bebop or bluegrass, Phil Woods or Ralph Stanley, Marty combines a 10th-fret choke, a flat-five, and an infectiously bouncy right hand to come up with some very compelling banjo music. His playing has graced such groups as Buck White, the Fiction Brothers, and Hazel Dickens.

At this point you can hear Marty to good advantage on the Fiction Brothers' album for Flying Fish, Kenny Kosek and Matt Glaser's scary double-fiddle album, *Hasty Lonesome,* on Rounder, and on Beet Records' acclaimed *Wretched Refuse.*

All of the licks included here are essentially of a jazz nature. The first is a sprawling four-measure G lick which encompasses a number of passing chords and some blues tonality towards the end.

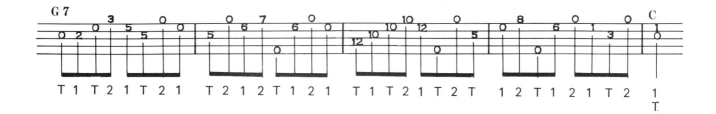

Your left hand will be quite occupied with this next one, but it's worth it.

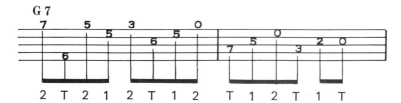

Famed jazz guitarist Pat Martino gives us:

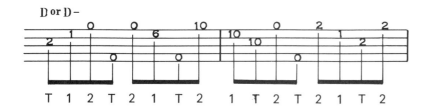

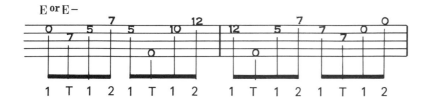

Marty refers to the following lick as a "pedal-point melodic run in D-minor." By this he refers to the chromatically descending line, starting with the first note, D, and stretching down to the second-string B. See if you can follow it.

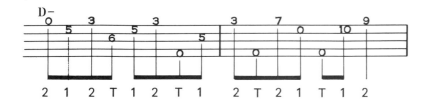

Finally this moveable concept run:

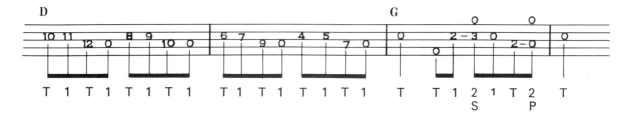

Peter Schwimmer

As of this writing, Peter's music is known only to a handful of aficionados in the Northeast (primarily the New York area) and the Northwest (the Tacoma-Vancouver corridor). He's done almost no touring, concentrating instead on playing local dates with a fine Bellingham, Washington band, Southfork. His recorded output is also small: one out-of-print album for a small Canadian company and a Southfork record put out by Grassroots Music (2737 N.E. 25th, Portland, Oregon). This, of course, has nothing to do with his level of musicianship.

Peter is at the pinnacle of his field in terms of versatility, technique, and feeling. He's not afraid to tackle the most ornamented of obscure fiddle tunes and then chase that down with a hard bebop rendering of Charlie Parker's "Donna Lee." The licks that follow will give you some small indication of his talent.

Here's a highly recommended way of moving from G to C.

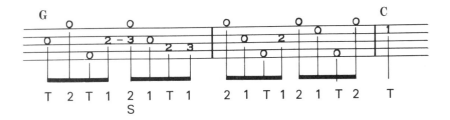

This next lick is a bit tricky in that you'll be hammering-on three notes without actually picking them.

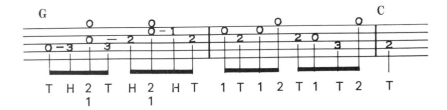

Here's one for the pantheon of contrary motion licks.

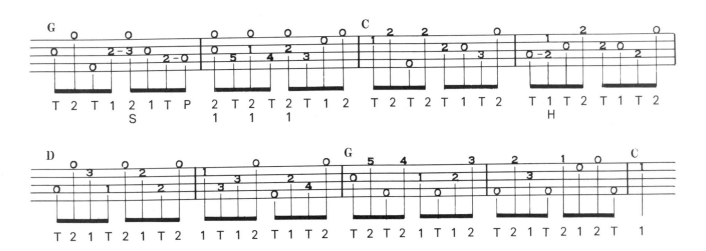

This is absolutely the hippest chorus "John Hardy" has ever had.

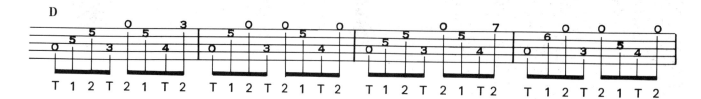

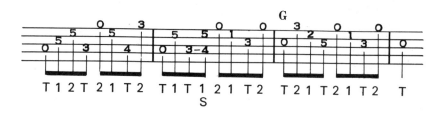

Finish with this delectable D-lick.

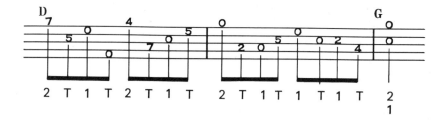

Dave Griffiths

I don't think there's anyone else in bluegrass who conjures notes on the banjo in quite the same way Dave does. A native of New Jersey, Mr. Griffiths had a proper Scruggs upbringing. But somewhere along the line he stepped out a dimension or two and the exciting results can be found on his *Workingman's Banjo* album (BMA Records, 36 Borden Place, Little Silver, New Jersey 07739).

Now let's tune into some of the licks that stamp Dave as a true original.

The first is certainly within the ballpark though it may give you a slightly different slant on this area of the fingerboard.

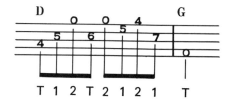

Dave suggested that this next lick could be played against a G or a D, but I think it sounds really nice against an F (perhaps for the chorus of "Salt Creek").

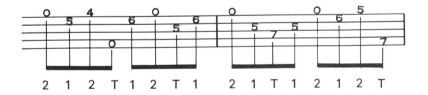

A lilting D-lick:

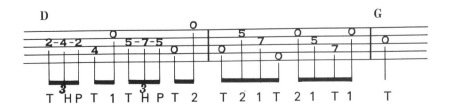

For these last two Dave came equipped with oxygen tanks and a chart to Alpha Centauri. The first may seem completely out there and yet after a few playings its logic should take hold and you'll see how completely satisfying it is.

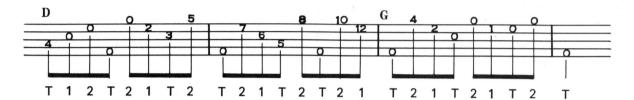

This final lick is an *outré* ending Dave put to his version of "Salt Creek" (available on *Workingman's Banjo*). To get the full chromatic effect this should be played at the speed of a tachyon particle.

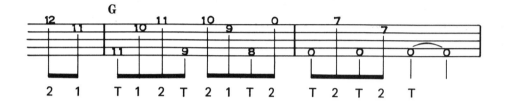

Endings

Finally, here are ten ending licks, ranging from the traditional to the modern.

We'll start with this ultra-prototypical Scruggs tag.

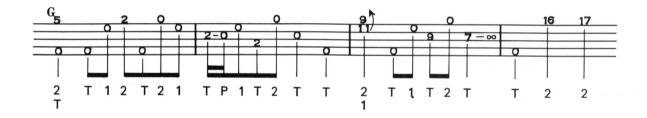

That can be extended by using the following compound ending, taken from the playing of Ralph Stanley.

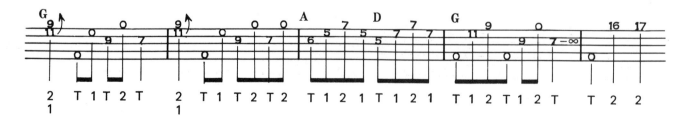

The haircut section of this next shave-and-a-haircut is a variation on a theme by Vic Jordan.

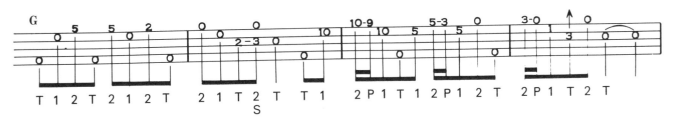

Jimmy Buchanan was one of Jim and Jesse's finest fiddlers. This is how he ended "Stony Creek."

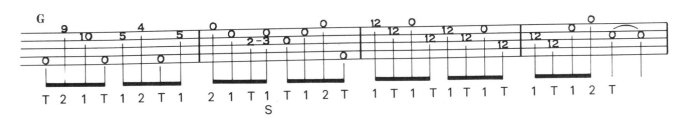

Here's a chromatic option.

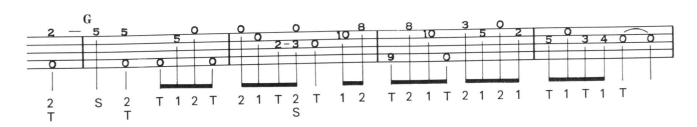

This is one of my personal favorites.

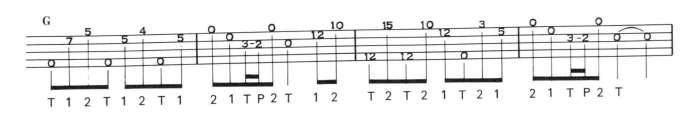

Two single stringers, the second of which features a low octave shave.

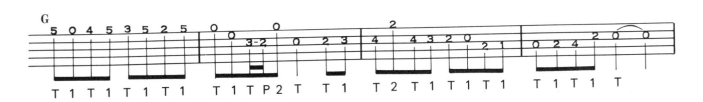

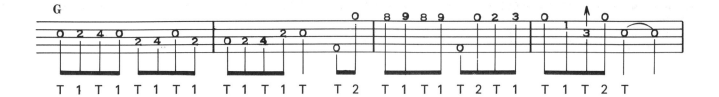

You may recognize this next one as common radio-station I.D. filler. Swing it, but keep the tempo down.

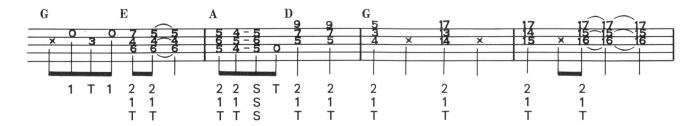

And:

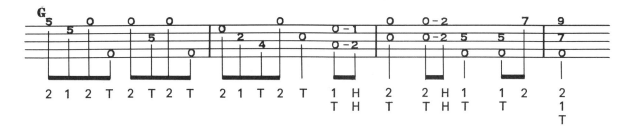

Thank you for coming.

Bill Keith, Tony Trischka, and Bela Fleck

Periodicals

If you only subscribe to one magazine this year, make sure it's
    Banjo Newsletter
    Box 364
    Greensboro, Maryland 21639

Hub and Nancy Nitchie have filled the pages of this monthly with bountiful tabs, in-depth interviews, regular columns, and a generous dosage of love and care. From beginning to advanced. This is highly recommended!

Also of interest is:
    International Banjo
    P.O. Box 328
    Kissimmee, Florida 32741

International Banjo covers both the five-string and tenor/plectrum market in a slick format that belies its downhome subject matter. Another good source for tabs and general banjo info.

For an overall bluegrass perspective don't miss the originial . . .
    Bluegrass Unlimited
    Box 111
    Broad Run, Virginia 22014

Frets magazine is a fine acoustic-music publication which delves into banjo consciousness at least once or twice each issue.
    Frets
    Box 28836
    San Diego, California 92128

Hot Licks in the 21st century (actually a participant in the 1981 Philadelphia Mummers' Parade)

Many people have a hard time learning music from the printed page. To clear up this problem, I've recorded a tape featuring most of the licks found in this book. Each lick will be played first slowly, and then up to speed. For complete information write:

Homespun Tapes
Box 694
Woodstock, New York 12498